Sutezou and Yukiko Kawabata

THE SEA IN THE MORNING

My grandfather's war memories

Keepsake House

Copyright © 2025 by Sutezou Kawabata and Yukiko Kawabata

Originally written in Japanese by Sutezou Kawabata.
Translated and rewritten in English by Yukiko Kawabata.
Cover and internal illustrations by Yukiko Kawabata

All rights reserved.
No portion of this book may be reproduced, published, performed in any form or by any means without prior written permission from the publisher or the author.

The illustrations are artistic impressions and are not intended to reflect complete historical accuracy.

For privacy reasons, some names may have been changed.

A catalogue record for this book is available from the National Library of Australia

ISBN 978-1-7643114-0-3 (paperback)
ISBN 978-1-7643114-1-0 (e-book)

www.keepsakehouse.com.au

Keepsake House

To Kai and Asa

Introduction

My grandfather, Sutezou Kawabata, often talked about 'the war'. Not in a serious, sit-down kind of way. His stories would just come up here and there, in the middle of everyday life – on the way to the beach, while circling the car park at the mall, or when we were sitting around with tea and snacks, watching TV.

He finished writing his war memoir in 1996, just before I left Japan to study overseas. I was probably 15 or 16 at the time. I don't remember the exact moment he gave it to me. He didn't make a big deal out of it, but I knew it mattered to him. He wanted his grandchildren to know what he had been through.

This was before the days of the internet and file sharing. All I had was a printed copy that had been typed up on an old word processor, not the kind of computer we use today. I packed it away and for many years, every time I relocated cities and countries, it stayed with me.

Now that I have children of my own, I feel the need to keep his story alive. My kids don't speak or read Japanese, so I decided to translate my grandfather's memoir into English, using words they could understand.

Here's something interesting: I married an American man. Our children are half-American – the same country my grandfather was once fighting against.

Even more surprising, my husband's grandfather served in the US Navy during the war. He was even stationed in the Philippines. It's possible he took part in the air raids my grandfather experienced.

My grandfather passed away before I met my husband. I often wonder what he would think about me marrying an American, and about his great-grandchildren being part of both sides of history.

The Americans were his 'enemy' but I never sensed any bitterness in him. What I did notice was a deep resentment towards his own country, for putting young, innocent men through such a torturous experience. I think he would actually be quite amused to find out who I married.

I wish I could ask him.

But for now, here is his story.

Yukiko Kawabata

1
Prologue

It has been over fifty years since the day I returned home from my final battleground, Mindanao in the Philippines, on the 25th of November 1945.

I can still remember the four years I spent in the war – between my enlistment in 1942 and my return in 1945 – as if it were yesterday. Those four years feel like they make up half of my 71 years of life.

Though what we went through in the war was atrocious, it has become part of the irreplaceable, invaluable history of who I am. That I made it back alive was nothing short of a miracle. In fact, it was one miracle after another.

Last year marked the 50th anniversary of the annual memorial service for our division. Now, the friends I fought beside are reaching the end of their lives. Our health is failing, and we no longer have many chances to talk about what we went through together. Even I find my memories fading at times.

At the very least, I want to record the memories that I can recall at this moment.

4th of January 1996

2
Enlistment

It all began in June 1941. I attended the draft examinations at the Asahi-Ku municipal office in Osaka, where I lived. I was 20 years old.

I passed with a grade Class II, B-1. Even though it was not the highest grade, I was still called up to join the military. This was because the war had worsened and they needed as many men as possible to fight for the country. In the past, during more peaceful times, only the Class I-A draftees were called up. Class I-A meant they had perfect health and strength. It was everyone's dream to receive the Class I-A.

My childhood friend from the same neighbourhood, Toshio Hashimoto, also attended the test. Sadly, he was suffering from pulmonary tuberculosis when he arrived for the draft examination. One of the physical tests involved lifting sandbags, but Toshio was too weak to move them. The examiner shouted cruelly, "Such a burden on the country. You should die straight away!" Toshio was given a Class IV-D grade, which meant he failed. He died not long after, on a hot summer day.

In October, I received an official notice from the ward office.

From that day, everything about my life took a turn, and the most miserable four years of my life began. I continued working at my regular job until two days before the enlistment, but I used all my spare time to mentally and physically prepare for what was ahead.

The day before my enlistment, my family, relatives and friends all gathered to celebrate at my parents' home. We spent the afternoon and evening sharing food and stories, cherishing what could be our last time together.

On the 1st of February, we rose at dawn to attend the enlistment celebration in town. A large crowd had gathered to see us off. We stepped up onto the stage and made our pledges to serve our country with honour. People cheered and shouted "Banzai!" – which literally means 'ten thousand years' and implies a wish for the Emperor of Japan to live a long life. They also offered words of support and encouragement. We boarded a tram, transferred to the Hanwa (railway) Line, arriving at the barrack gate of the 4th Field Artillery Regiment in Shinodayama much earlier than scheduled.

Each new recruit was allowed to bring one family member to help take home any personal belongings. My father, Kamejiro, came with me. After receiving our military uniforms and getting changed into them, we handed our everyday clothes to our family members to take back home.

We were then divided into our companies and taken to the barracks at the Shinodayama Training Grounds. I was placed in the Second Company. We had a bath and a meal under the supervision of the unit director. Our life as soldiers had officially begun.

3
Departure

Our daily training began the next day. We also visited the Kaneoka Military Hospital twice for health checks. After five days, our families were allowed to visit us.

Not long after, we were assigned to the 34th Field Artillery Regiment, part of the 34th Division, which was based in central China, around the city called Nanchang. Our departure was approaching. We kept training every morning, but our families came to see us almost every afternoon.

However, from the 8th of February, family visits were no longer allowed. Everyone suspected that our departure was imminent and the tension grew.

Early in the morning on the 11th of February, we had a departure ceremony. We left the barracks carrying only a few items: a sword, a field pack, a water bottle, a blanket and a tent. We took the Hanwa Line to Tennoji, switched onto the Japanese National Railway Line[1], heading to Suita Marshalling Yard. From there, we boarded a special military train to Hiroshima.

Our departure was technically supposed to be a secret. However, we were surprised to find an overflowing crowd of people gathered on the opposite platform while we were waiting for the train at Tennoji Station. Among them, I spotted my parents, my siblings, and my brother-in-law. Each of them held a cloth-wrapped bundle, called a *furoshiki*. They were trying to find a way to pass them to us, but were on the far side of the tracks and we couldn't get close.

My mother died about a year later, while I was on duty in China. I also noticed Suga, my oldest sister,

---

1. Now known as the Japan Railways (JR) Group

wasn't there. I found out later that she had suddenly become very ill and passed away that same day.

Eventually, we walked across the station bridge towards the platform. Luckily, I had the chance to walk past my family and, seizing that split second, my brother-in-law quickly passed me the *furoshiki*. There wasn't even time to exchange words.

We boarded the train and arrived at the Suita Marshalling Yard, where we changed to a military train heading to Hiroshima. All the windows were covered with the blackout coverings, closed off from the outside world.

Inside the train, we were packed like canned sardines. I kept thinking about the *furoshiki* my family gave me. When no-one was watching, I secretly opened it to have a peek.

I was shocked when I saw what was inside. Even though food was scarce during wartime, my family had somehow packed all sorts of special items. Two of them really stood out: a tin of whiskey-filled chocolates, called whiskey bonbons, and a box of *botamochi* – rice cakes covered in sweet red bean paste (*anko*).

Getting hands on something sweet like *botamochi* was incredibly rare back then. I imagined my family working together to make them on short notice, using precious sugar they must have obtained through special means while everyone else sacrificed. I felt tears welling up as I imagined the scene with everyone involved in making them. I didn't want to share them with anyone. I waited for a chance to eat them all alone, but the train was too crowded.

We finally reached Hiroshima around midnight. When we arrived, we marched for about two hours through the city of Hiroshima to Ujina Port. We decided to rest until the departure of the ship in the morning, but the harbour at midnight was frigid. Some soldiers gathered wood to warm up by the bonfire.

I didn't join them. Instead, I slipped away with my *furoshiki* and found a quiet place to eat the *botamochi* all by myself. The *anko* was packed all the way into the corners of the box and every bite felt like a treasure. It had been so long since I'd tasted something that delicious.

As the eastern sky started to lighten, we wrapped straw around our shoes so we wouldn't slip as we boarded the cargo ship.

Soon after, we set sail from Ujina Port, heading for Shanghai.

The last time I saw my mother – in the crowd at Tennoji Station.

4
The Voyage to China

I don't recall exactly how many days it took us to sail to Shanghai. There wasn't much to do on the ship, except for the roll calls and a couple of emergency drills. Most of the time, we just talked among ourselves and slowly got to know one another.

After several days, we finally arrived safely in Shanghai. From there, we boarded another ferry and began our journey up Yangtze River towards Jiujiang, a city farther inland.

The rooms of this ship were divided into two levels, and the ceilings were so low we couldn't even stand up straight inside.

By then, over half a month had passed since we had left home. Everyone was starting to feel homesick.

Living under strict army rules – and eating army meals – made us all think about food from home. The supplied meals weren't enough and we were constantly hungry. Sometimes at night, when the Chinese cooks had gone to sleep, we sneaked into the kitchen and ate some leftover charred rice.

The Yangtze River was much bigger than I had imagined. The landscape along the riverbanks of this continent felt so vast in contrast to the familiar scenery of the island nation of Japan. I saw some large old cities like Nanjing and Anqing as we passed by. The houses by the river looked so foreign, and huge birds with tattered tails flew over the villages. It made me realise just how far from Japan we really were.

After a few days, we reached Jiujiang. We got off the boat and stayed in a dormitory for the night – our first camp on the mainland. The next day, we took the Nanxun Railway, heading to Nanchang, where our Second Company was based.

While on the train out of Jiujiang, we suddenly stopped near a small lake. An officer told us that guerrilla fighters had destroyed part of the track, so the train couldn't go any further.

We had to get off and carry all our belongings along the edge of the small lake. First, we took off our personal gear and left it by the side of the road. Then we had to carry the rest of the load across. One of the hardest things to carry were the sixty-kilogram bags of horse feed. We were ordered to carry them on our backs, but it was incredibly difficult.

As I struggled to lift one onto my back, an officer behind me kicked me hard in the hip and knocked me over. That was the first time I truly realised how harsh and unfair life in the army could be – and how powerless I really was.

Afterward, when I returned to retrieve my belongings, I discovered my raincoat had been stolen. I didn't want to be left without one, so I reluctantly stole someone else's. It was the first time I had ever stolen anything. It was also the first time I realised how common theft was among soldiers.

Eventually, another train came to pick us up and, by the evening, we had arrived at Nanchang Station.

Some of the soldiers from our company greeted us with horses. The officers rode the horses, and the rest of us marched towards the barracks on foot. A wide river flowed near the station, and we had to cross a long bridge before continuing on. It was dark by the time we finally arrived.

The barracks was a three-storey building made of bricks. It used to be a large hospital, but had been damaged – probably through war activity.

It was already late at night. The company commander welcomed us with a speech, which was followed by the introductions of other officers. To celebrate our arrival, we were treated with *sake* (Japanese rice wine), which we drank from the lids of our mess kits, and a dinner of *sekihan* – a special sticky red rice dish usually served on celebratory occasions. Then, all the new recruits and the other soldiers went to sleep together in the same large room.

5
Nanchang Barracks

On our first day at the Nanchang Barracks, we spent the whole day familiarising ourselves with life at the barracks.

After a few days, we were divided into groups. There was a group of fifteen people judged to be not physically fit enough to keep up with the tough army duties. This group was called the 'Health Soldier Group'. I was included in this group too because I was judged to be slightly lacking in strength and stamina. We were excused from duties such as night shifts, stable duty and guard duty – tasks that new recruits usually had to do.

One of our duties in the Health Soldier Group was to collect grass for horse feed. Each morning and evening, we'd go outside the barracks carrying a straw sack and a sickle to cut the grass. Many of the others came from farming areas like Nara and Wakayama, so they were fast and skilled at cutting. I wasn't, and I had a hard time keeping up because I'd never done that kind of work before.

After some time, all the new recruits were given an official role in the military, such as gunner, coachman, spotter, or communications operator[2]. I was chosen to be a coachman, which meant I would work with horses. My training began.

---

2. The 'coachman' handled and took care of the horses that pulled the carts carrying important supplies, such as food, ammunition and equipment. The 'gunner' operated and maintained guns, cannons or other artillery systems. The 'spotter' observed targets, assessed wind and distance, and communicated this information to the shooters (snipers) to aid with accuracy. The 'communications operators' maintained communication between units and headquarters, and operated systems including radio, telegraph, field telephone and signal flags.

Once training had started, there were no special exceptions for being in the Health Soldier Group. I now had to take care of the horses and stables every single day – rain or shine – as well as having horseriding training every morning and afternoon. Eventually, they removed me from the Health Soldier Group, and I had to follow the same schedule as the other soldiers. This included training, cleaning, guard duties and other responsibilities. Our days were filled with backbreaking tasks.

Life as a new recruit was also mentally unpleasant. A soldier who was even one day more senior than you could act superior and boss you around. If something of yours was stolen, you got punished for being careless – but if you stole something from someone else, it was considered clever and even praised.

Hence, many of the new recruits aimed to pass the First Period Examinations, which were the first step towards becoming an officer. I managed to pass and was promoted to First Class Private. Not long after that, however, my health began to deteriorate.

6
Missed Promotion

I was diagnosed with jaundice and beriberi[3]. Because of that, even though I had studied very hard every night after my exhausting training and duties, I was no longer allowed to take the test to become an officer.

I was sent to the military hospital in Nanchang, then transferred to Jiujiang. Eventually, I ended up in a hospital in Wuchang. I was there for about three months.

---

3. 'Jaundice' is a condition that indicates liver problems. It causes the skin and eyes to turn yellow due to a buildup of bilirubin in the blood. 'Beriberi' is a disease caused by thiamine (vitamin B1) deficiency. It often leads to weakness, nerve problems and heart issues.

By the time I had recovered and returned to my unit, most of my friends had passed the exams and been promoted. I was disappointed and felt ashamed of being a 'hospital soldier'.

My first job after leaving the hospital was bathhouse duty. Every morning, I would go collect firewood, clean the bath, fix leaks in the bathtub and prepare the bathwater. The firewood wasn't provided – I had to go find it myself.

While exercising the horses in the morning, I would look for bits of wood and then go back to collect them later in the day. If I couldn't find enough small pieces, I had the horses pull back large fallen logs, like old power poles, from the roadside. I used a pickaxe to break them into usable firewood.

The bathhouse itself had been handmade by some older soldiers using whatever materials they could find. Over a hundred people used the bath regularly, so it would often leak. Whenever it did, we stuffed rags into the cracks to keep the water from spilling out.

Not long after, some older cooks were caught stealing food and selling it to local people. They were put in detention and I was chosen to take their place in the kitchen. Being a cook meant I had enough to eat, but I didn't want to be stuck in that role forever. As soon as the original cooks were released, I pleaded for a transfer.

I got one, but it wasn't what I expected.

I was immediately assigned to 'officer meal duty', which was serving food to all the officers. Some of them were unusual characters – loud, bossy and full of ego. I found this work humiliating, but stayed focused and determined. I promised myself I would do everything I could to get promoted to upper first-class private at the next selection, and eventually qualify for the First Captain exams later.

7
Rear Horse Coachman

Besides our daily duties, we spent most of our time in horseriding training and caring for the horses. This went on until the first big exam for field artillery coachmen.

At first, we trained one-on-one with our horses at the riding grounds. To stop ourselves from falling off, we often looped the stirrups over the front of the saddle and gripped tightly with our legs. This caused the skin on the inside of our knees to rub raw and bleed. Our long underwear would turn red with blood, and it became very painful. Once we passed the basic lessons, we began learning how to ride side-by-side in formation.

Coachmen in the field artillery had a tough job. We had to control six horses at once to pull heavy equipment like limbers (two-wheeled carts for moving artillery), ammunition carriers, measuring instruments and even the gun carriages themselves. The six horses were grouped in pairs – two front horses, two middle horses and two rear horses. This setup was called 'six-in-hand'.

All the horses had to move in perfect coordination to safely pull the heavy gear to its destination.

Attached to the front of the equipment cart was a long metal shaft that was about the length of a horse. The last pair of horses – the rear horses – had metal chains attached from their neck straps to this shaft. That meant only the rear horse coachmen were responsible for steering the shaft and keeping the cart steady.

The unsealed roads were bumpy so the front wheels of the cart bounced violently, shaking the shaft in every direction. It took great skill and strength to control it. For that reason, rear horses were larger and wore stronger, more complicated harnesses. The rear coachman's job was the most important, but also the most dangerous.

People used to say: "Stylish front horse, mediocre middle horse and daredevil rear horse coachman."

Becoming a rear coachman was the path to being promoted to upper first-class private. But to qualify, you had to prove your skill not just in riding, but also in taking care of the horses and keeping their gear perfectly maintained. You also had to have a spotless record on all your army duties.

If you were a coachman, the stable was your second home. No matter how tired you were, you were expected to spend almost all your free time there, looking after the horses and their equipment.

8
Yichang Operations

It was May of 1943, and I was on duty at the guardhouse.

Our company was short on people because many had been transferred, hospitalised or sent off to officer training school. This meant we all had to take on more duties, more often. Sometimes, I would finish a full shift of guard duty and then be put straight onto stable duty without any rest. There were many times I couldn't sleep for more than two nights in a row.

Guard duty shifts followed a repeating cycle of 'guard, rest and standby' every hour. At night, one guard would stand watch from inside a pillbox[4], while the other patrolled the area behind the building. The one who finished their shifts could nap in a small room at the back of the guardhouse.

That night, I overheard a conversation between the guard commander and a corporal. They were talking about an upcoming military operation in Yichang, and that we would be part of it.

Sure enough, two or three days later, we were officially told we would be joining the Yichang operations.

Our mission was to provide transport support by using our horses to help carry supplies. Our team included about thirty soldiers, led by Second Lieutenant Matsumoto, with Sergeant Yamada and Corporal Okuda as part of the group.

---

4. A 'pillbox' was a small, strong shelter made of concrete where soldiers could hide and shoot at enemies.

We left Nanchang and travelled by train to Jiujiang. There, we had medical check-ups and were given new equipment for the mission. From Jiujiang, we boarded a ship to Hankou, where we had a short rest. Hankou was incredibly hot. As we marched through the streets, we saw local people sleeping outdoors on beds to escape the heat inside their homes.

From Hankou, we took a day-long train ride to a small town called Changkoufu, arriving on a drizzly evening. We took some peas from a nearby field and cooked pea rice in our mess kits for dinner. That night, we slept on the dirt floors of local civilian homes.

The next day, in the rain, we began our march towards Yichang. Along the way, we passed through a city called Yingcheng. While passing through, someone in our group caught a wild rabbit. We cooked it and made rabbit soup – a rare and delicious treat.

At one point, we ran out of clean water and had to drink warm water from a rice field, even though water buffalo had been roaming around it. Another time, we reached a wide river and had to camp for the night before crossing. There was a tiny shed by the riverbank where many soldiers had stayed before us. It had barely enough space to lie down—but we were still glad to have shelter. It meant we could sleep without needing to set up a full camp.

9
Into the Mountains

After about a week of marching, we finally reached Yichang, a large city along the Yangtze River. Just like Nanchang, the city had many shops. We even spotted a few restaurants run by Japanese people.

A communications soldier named Koizumi came back to meet us. He had arrived a few days ahead of us, and told us about the situation at the frontline.

The wide Yangtze River became narrower at Yichang, making it easier to cross. Our plan was to cross the river at night under the cover of darkness. The frontline wasn't far from the riverbank. Koizumi told us that, even from a distance, you could hear the eerie rumble of enemy artillery – especially the deep thudding of trench mortars.

We stayed a day or two in Yichang, then headed to the river where we were split up onto different boats. I remember the river crossing only took about twenty minutes and we made it across safely that night. On the other side of the river, our forces had set up a military supply warehouse. We loaded up supplies there and began marching again, heading deeper into the mountains.

It was mountainous and rugged on this side of the river. As we climbed further inland, we began to hear the deep booms of trench mortars together with the higher-pitched crack of gunfire. That's when we knew we had reached the real front.

From then on, we marched day and night without proper rest. We marched in a moonless, pitch-black landscape, and had no idea what the land around us looked like. One night, we had to cross a raging river in total darkness. To make it worse, we had heard there was an enemy outpost nearby, so we couldn't make a sound. Surprisingly, the horses led the way. They could see better in the dark than we could. I had no idea where we were going – I just gripped the reins tightly, trusted the horse and followed. Somehow, I made it safely across the rapids, even though I couldn't really see or understand what was happening.

As part of the supply unit, we marched behind the main infantry. We moved along narrow mountain gorges, while the sounds of gunfire echoed all around us. Horses and soldiers alike had to walk through knee-deep water in the streambeds. The cliffs on both sides of us echoed the sounds of gunfire even louder, and bullets sometimes came so close they whistled past our ears. We eventually learned that high-pitched gunfire came from the enemy, while the duller sounds were from our own side.

Walking through water day and night wore out our rubber-soled socks and made the shoes fall off the horses' hooves. We waited until dawn so the farrier (the person who shoes the horses) could fix them. However, wet and damaged hooves made it difficult to get a proper fit.

Despite all of this, the marching didn't stop. During the daytime, we could see the team ahead of us. But at night, we had to follow their coded instructions, which they had left at key points along the path. Everyone was completely sleep-deprived from marching for days without proper rest.

At night, we only knew the march had stopped when we accidentally bumped into the horse in front of us. When that happened, we stopped too and took the chance to rest – standing up. Many of us grabbed the tails of the horses in front so we would feel them move if they started walking again. That way, even if we fell asleep, we wouldn't get left behind.

The march went on like this, day after day, through the steep mountain valleys. As dawn approached, we followed the movement of the horses in front of us, but soon realised we had lost contact with our team ahead.

It turned out that the team had moved on while some of the soldiers in front of us were dozing. When the person ahead of us finally woke up and started marching, he accidentally followed a different stream at a fork in the path. None the wiser, the rest of us followed him – into the wrong gorge.

10
Ambushed

The sun had fully risen and we were finally able to see where we were. That's when we realised something terrifying – we had wandered straight into enemy territory. In the distance, we could see pillboxes built into the mountains.

We quickly took cover in a small shed in a rice field, hidden in the shadow of the mountain. With our horses tied up behind the shed, we tried to stay quiet as we ate some rice from our mess kits.

Suddenly, there was a burst of machine-gun fire. It was aimed directly at our shed. The enemy had spotted us.

There were seven or eight of us in total, all under the command of Sergeant Yamada. He immediately ordered us to retreat. We tried to escape but many of the horses' shoes had come off, making their movement slow and difficult. The enemy must have noticed our retreat because their attack became even more aggressive.

I don't clearly remember how I got away. I just focused on staying alive as I pulled my horse along behind me, moving from rock to rock, and tree root to tree root, trying to stay hidden. But the gunfire didn't stop.

Suddenly, Sergeant Yamada shouted, "Snipers! Fire!" He pointed towards a shadow in the trees. I turned to where he was pointing, saw a human-shaped outline and quickly pulled the rifle from my back. I fired a few shots in that direction but couldn't stop to see what happened. I kept retreating, climbing over a large rock while dragging my horse by the reins.

The horse was struggling badly. As I pulled, the enemy's bullets sparked on the bedrock by my feet. I realised I was in serious danger. If I stayed, I'd be killed so I let go of the reins and hid behind the rock by myself – without the horse.

I kept moving, crawling and running from one hiding place to the next, always listening for the next shot. Whenever I paused, the firing would stop. And every time I got up to move again, the bullets followed. It felt like the enemy could hear my every footstep.

Somehow, after climbing several hills and crossing several gorges, I finally reached an area out of enemy range. One by one, all seven or eight of us regrouped. I had no idea how the others had escaped. Amazingly, no-one had been killed and no-one was seriously injured.

As night fell, we found another small shed in a rice field and took turns standing guard. We were cold, wet and exhausted.

Then the hunger hit. We hadn't eaten anything close to a real meal in a long time. We spotted a wandering calf nearby and, driven by hunger, we killed it and ate the meat raw.

Even though I hadn't slept properly in days, I couldn't fall asleep that night. I kept imagining lights moving in the distance and thought I heard footsteps approaching. It was one of the longest nights of my life but as the sky began to brighten, with the mountains looking peaceful and green again, and the river flowing quietly beside us, it was as if nothing had happened.

Later that day, a plane flew overhead and dropped a communication tube. Inside was a message telling us the position of our main unit and the latest battle information. We quickly headed out to rejoin them.

By the time we arrived, the main forces were already in heavy combat. During that battle, First Class Private Yoshikazu Nishida, who had joined the army the same year as me, was killed by enemy gunfire.

Eventually, the enemy pulled back and we were ordered to return to where we had first come under fire. We needed to recover the horses that had been lost during the ambush.

To my surprise, the horse I'd let go during the escape was still alive, peacefully eating grass. My relief didn't last long, though. As a field artillery coachman, it was my responsibility to never abandon a horse in battle, and I was severely scolded and punished.

11
Returning to Nanchang

In the battles we faced deep in the mountains, it was common to attack and then turn around to return, not proceeding any further once the enemy had moved back to a certain point. After two or three days, we reached the crossing point of the Yangtze River again and made it safely across.

We marched for a few more days before arriving at a small village, where we set up camp. Just as we thought the operation was over, we received word that some of our troops were stuck on the other side of the river and needed help.

Even though I'd hoped to return to my home unit and finally have some rest, I was ordered to go back across the river – this time as a cavalry messenger under

Corporal Okuda. I was disappointed by the sudden news and frustrated that I had to go back into the fight.

That night, we crossed the river again. Many boats were lined up along the riverbank, and we hopped from boat to boat to reach the far side. Just before the last boat left, more soldiers boarded. One of them, a communications soldier carrying gear on both shoulders, slipped between two boats and fell into the river. He never resurfaced. The river's surface was calm, but I had heard the currents below were fast and strong. He was probably already worn out from marching for so many days. Watching him disappear shook me, and I knew I had to be extra careful.

After we crossed, Corporal Okuda and I marched through farmland with the rest of the infantry. We came across some minor resistance fighters, but they weren't well-equipped and we pushed them back without much trouble. Since it was just the two of us from the supply team, and we didn't have horses this time, the march was relatively easy, aside from those small clashes.

The unit followed a path alongside a large lake. Every now and then, we caught beautiful views of the water. After a while, we reached a large town called Jianli, where we rested for a few days. There was a friendly military unit already stationed there with a well-developed barracks.

After leaving Jianli, we marched again before boarding a ship at the port town of Shashi, and sailing down the Yangtze River back to Hankou. There, we finally rejoined our main supply unit.

We stepped off the boat and walked through the city to reach the barracks. I'll never forget how Japanese civilians living in Hankou came out and cheered as we passed by.

Once we reached Hankou, our mission officially ended. By the time we returned to our home base in Nanchang, it was already the middle of a hot summer.

Upon our arrival in Nanchang, we found that the 34th Field Artillery Regiment had been dissolved, and a new one – the 30th Field Artillery Regiment – had already been created and moved to Pyongyang, in North Korea.

I laughed out loud when I found out I'd been mistakenly listed as 'killed in action' during the Yichang operation! But I was proud to learn I'd been promoted to upper first-class private.

Although the entire operation only lasted about two months, it was full of danger, hardship, and close calls. I'll never forget how a split-second decision – like going the wrong way in the mountains – almost had all of us surrounded and attacked.

I can still remember clearly what was going through my mind during those terrifying moments – hiding behind the rocks and trying to decide when to make my next move. Everything felt unreal, my mind kept going back to my family back home.

12
Nanchang to Pyongyang

After the Yichang operation ended, many of our horses had infections, sore hooves and other health problems. We handed them over to a horse hospital, said our goodbyes and got ready to leave Nanchang.

I'd only been stationed there for a short time but I already felt a sense of attachment to the place. I found myself missing the training grounds where we'd pushed ourselves every day as new recruits, and also missing the stables where we'd fed and cared for our horses every morning and night.

As a result of the long and exhausting marches, irregular routines and unhygienic conditions during the battle, my health had deteriorated. Around the time we departed Nanchang, I was struck by a severe case of diarrhoea.

The journey to Pyongyang was supposed to be simple. We didn't have to haul horses or equipment this time, which should have made it easier – but for me, it wasn't. I had such a miserable time due to my poor health.

First, we took the Nanxun Railway to Jiujiang, then boarded a ship to Nanjing. From there, we crossed the Yangtze River to a city called Pukou. After that, we travelled by train through Xuzhou, Jinan and Shenyang, finally crossing the Yalu River into Pyongyang.

I did not have the chance to receive treatment for my diarrhoea before we left and it made the train ride between Pukou and Pyongyang incredibly difficult. The worst part was that we were riding in a freight train boxcar, which didn't have a bathroom. Every time the train made a sudden stop – usually at a traffic light or for some unknown reason – I had to quickly jump out and relieve myself.

It was a risky manoeuvre: holding onto part of the train with one hand, trying to pull down my pants and underwear with the other, and always keeping an eye out for when the train might start moving again. If it did, I had to jump back on immediately – sometimes mid-squat. We travelled like this for days.

By the time we finally arrived in Pyongyang, I was in terrible shape. My body had grown very weak and I could barely stand. After a medical check-up, I was sent straight to Pyongyang First Army Hospital.

The doctors diagnosed me with dysentery and fluid in my right lung. I was ordered to stay in the hospital for treatment.

13
Hospital in Pyongyang

At first, I couldn't sleep at all. I was probably overwhelmed from the stress and exhaustion of everything I'd been through. Little by little, though, I began to feel more settled and my appetite started coming back.

As my health improved, I was moved into a large room with about forty other patients.

Most of the others in the room had never been to the frontlines. Because I'd just returned from a real battlefield, and was a field artillery upper first-class private, I was given a lot of respect. They even put me in charge of the room as 'room captain'.

One day, a very important visitor came to inspect the hospital – Army General Seishirō Itagaki, commander of the Japanese Korean Army. As captain, I led the others during the inspection. When the General walked into our room, he stopped in front of my bed, picked up my diary and asked me some questions about where I'd become sick during the operation.

Of course, I'd sent word to my family as soon as I was hospitalised. Not long after, a small parcel arrived. It was from my brother-in-law from the Minamino family. Inside the package was a tin full of *mochi* (rice cakes). I knew they'd made the *mochi* as soon as they heard I'd survived the battlefield and made it to Korea, so they'd started to grow a little green mould. I didn't care. I couldn't waste their effort and, besides, I was so touched and homesick I had to eat them. When no-one was watching, I quietly cooked and ate them at the fire pit near the bath. Even without soy sauce or salt, they tasted amazing.

By the end of that first month, my health had improved a lot. Around the middle of summer, I received a letter saying that my older brother from the Nakajima family, and my second brother from the Yasuma family were both coming to visit me in Pyongyang.

It felt like a dream when they walked into my hospital room. I didn't even know what to say. I'd recovered enough to sit up and talk, and just seeing them again meant the world to me.

We talked about many things, and they shared news and stories from home. Strangely, though, they said nothing about my mother.

I started to feel uneasy. She was never robust in health, but I was too scared to ask. Deep down, I already knew the answer.

Finally, I gathered the courage to ask. It was just as I'd feared – she had passed away.

I thought I was ready to hear it, but when they said the words my vision went pitch black. I could barely process it.

Then came another shock – my oldest sister had also died. I'd suspected something about our mother but hadn't imagined receiving this news about my sister, not even in my worst dreams.

It turned out she'd been in critical condition on the very day I left for Nanchang. I remembered seeing my family at Tennoji Station as I switched trains – everyone except my sister. I had wondered about it then but now realised that she may have passed away while I was eating the *botamochi* my family had given me at the pier in Hiroshima.

My brothers stayed in Pyongyang for two or three nights and visited me at the hospital each day. Because I was room captain and an upper first-class private, I didn't have to worry about the people around me. I was able to enjoy my time with them in peace, despite the sorrow in my heart.

The city of Pyongyang was split in two by the Taedong River, which flowed just north of the city centre. Most military units, including the division headquarters, were based on the north side of the river in an area called Chueul. The Pyongyang First Army

Hospital, where I was recovering, was also located in this area.

A large iron bridge crossed the river. On the south side of the bridge was the city's old town, where there was a Houkoukan – a special accommodation building for Japanese military visitors. That's where my brothers stayed during their visit.

The four days they spent with me passed by like a dream. Then, just like that, they had to return home.

At that time, the war situation wasn't going well. The newspapers at the hospital reported that Italy, one of Japan's allies, had surrendered. That news was worrying enough, but then things became even scarier.

Just three or four days after my brothers left Pyongyang, I read in the newspaper that the *Konron Maru*, a ferry that sailed between the Japanese port of Shimonoseki and Busan in Korea, had been sunk by an American submarine. I panicked. Based on their travel route, there was a real chance my brothers had been on that very boat.

I was deeply relieved when, a few days later, a letter arrived saying they were safe. As it turned out, they had made an unexpected stop in Seoul on the way back, and that change in plan meant they had avoided the attack entirely.

From then on, life in the hospital became much calmer. I shared a large room with many other recovering soldiers, most of whom were easygoing and fun to be around. Sometimes civilians and entertainers would visit us. On other days, we bought boxes of apples from the locals. We ate them, of course, but sometimes also used them at night for the little gambling games we played until the lights went out.

After a while, fully recovered from my illness and feeling healthy again, I decided to submit a request to return to duty. I asked the military doctor for permission to be discharged from the hospital and go back to serving.

14
Nude Run

I was released from the hospital and returned to duty. As I was now strong enough again to take on responsibilities, I was put in charge of the internal affairs corps, helping with the company's daily tasks and routines.

Autumn was near its end and, with winter approaching, the weather had become bitterly cold. One day, I returned late from the armoury to find that everyone else had already gone to take care of the evening stable duty; only the barracks guards and soldiers were still around.

Private Tokunaga, a kitchen worker whose bed was next to mine, walked in from the kitchen.

"Hey, Tokunaga!" I greeted him. "Is the bath ready?"

"Yeah, just finished heating it up," he replied.

I didn't feel like going to the stables that evening, so I grabbed my *tenugui* (a small hand towel) and headed straight for the bath.

In the changing room, I found my friend from the first squad, Shinichi Kawamura. He was already undressing. I called out to him. "Hey, you! Skipping stable duty too?"

He laughed. "You're one to talk!" he said.

Bath time in our regiment was managed by the kitchen staff and each company was given a set time to bathe. They would blow a bugle to announce when it was your turn. That day, our companies had been given the last slots, scheduled after dinner.

Even though it was not our turn yet, we climbed into the big warm bath. The sunlight coming through the window made the clear water shine. I leaned back, relaxing up to my neck, and sang a famous old song about a town known for its hot springs:

"Kusatsu is a good place, come once …"

Suddenly, footsteps echoed at the entrance and the weekly duty officer burst into the bathroom.

We jumped in surprise. But it was too late.

He barked, "Which company do you belong to?"

"Second Company, sir!" we responded.

"What time is your bath slot?"

"After dinner, when the bugle blows, sir!"

"Has the bugle sounded?"

"No sir, not yet."

"Then get out. Line up in front of the barracks!"

We scrambled to get dressed.

"No! As you are!" came the order.

Reluctantly, we removed our pants but left on our long underwear.

"I said no!" he barked again. "Naked! You may keep your shoes."

So there we were – two soldiers, completely naked, wearing only our barracks shoes, which looked like giant boats on our bare feet. Shivering, we lined up outside the bathhouse.

"Line up! Attention! You're going to run around the barracks! Right face! Double time. Go!"

We had no choice. We took off, running in the freezing late autumn air with the cold biting our bare skin.

As we neared the stables, we heard the dinner bugle blow. Soldiers from all the companies were marching back to the barracks in lines, singing cadences, and led by their sergeants.

And there we were – still running in circles around the base, completely naked except for our boots.

As they passed the weekly duty officer, he ordered the other soldiers, "Salute the weekly duty officer. Eyes right!"

And while they saluted and marched past him properly, we kept running, catching everyone's attention.

After one full lap, we were finally excused and allowed to go back to the barracks. Luckily, no senior officers were around that evening. If they had been, we might have been in serious trouble. Still, the teasing was endless.

"Hey! You guys looked fantastic out there!"

Even the next day, everyone was still laughing. Overnight, I'd become famous for our 'nude run'.

The 'nude run' with everyone looking on.

15

Preparing for the Southern Operations

Winter in North Korea was extreme—sometimes dropping to minus 28 degrees Celsius at night.

During this time, I was given many responsibilities. I worked guard duty, took part in the weekly shifts for upper first-class privates and often helped out at the stables. The duty I performed most often was serving at the armoury, where I worked as an assistant to the regiment's weapon committee.

Our regiment barracks were surrounded by pine-covered hills, with sloping paths that were great for morning horse exercises. I often controlled three or four horses at once and was later recognised as an excellent rear horse coachman during an equestrian competition held in those hills.

While on guard duty one day, I slipped on a frozen puddle behind the kitchen and fell hard. I couldn't get up because of my heavy winter gear and I only managed to stand with help from a fellow soldier.

Another time, I was dragging a heavy gun carriage down a snowy hill when I fell with the horses. One of the large rear horses fell on top of me, pinning me to the ground. I held onto the reins with all my strength and slid down the hill for ten or twenty metres. If I'd let go, I would've been crushed by the gun carriage behind me – a Type 91, 10 cm howitzer. It was a terrifying moment.

We also had regular drills at Taedong Barracks, which was a half-day march away. I went to almost all of them.

All these activities were in preparation for expected battles in northern Manchuria. We thought we'd be deployed there soon. At the time, even the uniform warehouse was full of winter clothing, which fit with those plans.

As the frigid February and March passed and spring was approaching in Pyongyang, things started to change.

Suddenly, we heard rumours about a shift to Southern Operations. Then the clothing warehouse switched its inventory to summer uniforms and our daily bulletins after roll call started giving updates about the southern front. We realised that our unit might be heading to a very different battlefield than we'd thought.

In late April it became official – we were told we'd take part in the Southern Operations. The armoury became busy with preparations as more and more new draftees began arriving at the barracks.

Among the new arrivals were older veterans who'd already been honourably discharged a year or two before. There were also 'filler' recruits – some of whom were older, had minor physical disabilities or looked less fit. Watching them arrive, I sensed something was wrong. It felt like the army was desperate to find enough soldiers.

On the 29th of April 1944, we received the official mobilisation order.

By then, I was mentally prepared. Deep down, I knew this deployment to Southern Operations might be the end of the road for me.

After the order came, our morning assemblies and drills changed focus. We began training for emergencies at sea just in case our troop transport ship was attacked. We practised jumping out windows and escaping from the upper floors using rope ladders.

Finally, on the 6th of May, we had our departure ceremony in front of the barracks and left for Pyongyang Station.

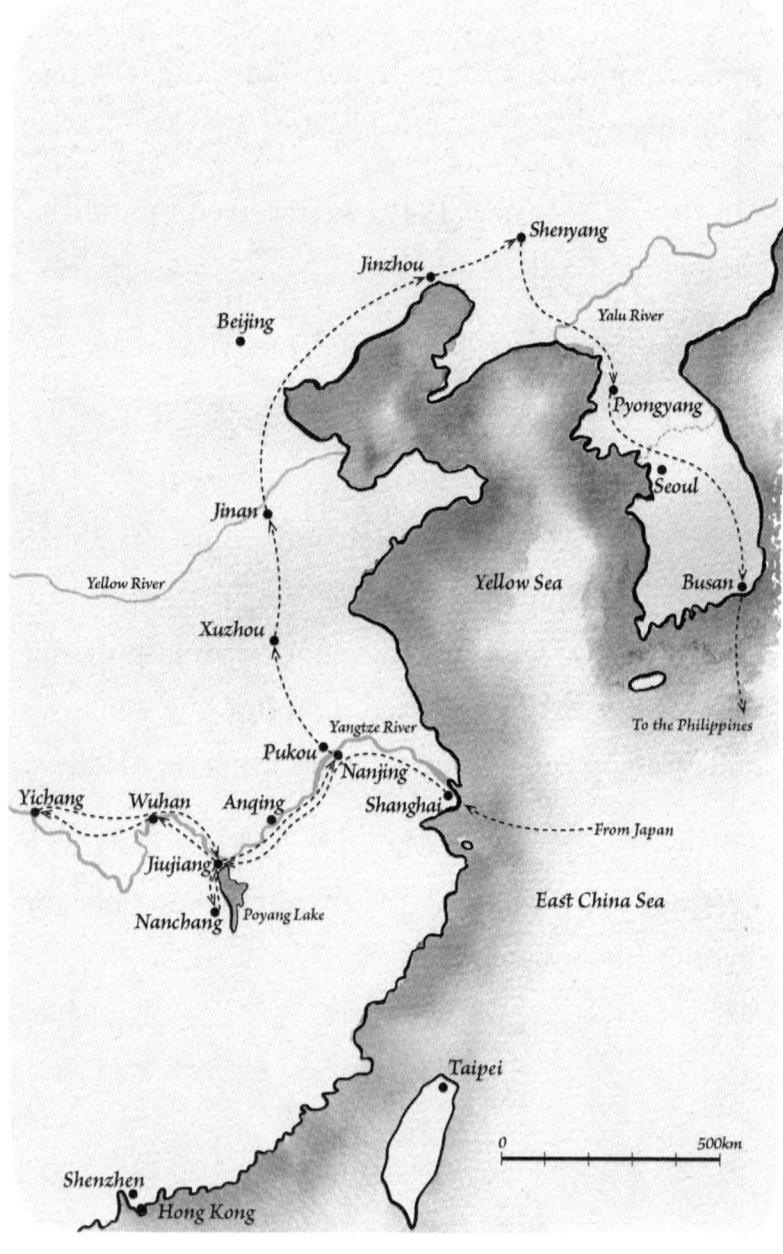

Our movements from Japan to Nanchang to Pyongyang

16

The Journey to the Philippines

I was assigned to the first squad as a rear horse coachman. My two draft horses were named Rintsu and Rensetsu. Our gun carriage was a Type 38, 75 mm field gun, requiring a team of four horses – two in the front and two in the back.

When I was a new recruit, I'd always trained with six-horse teams. These had front, middle and rear pairs. Four horses without a middle pair didn't feel stable to me. It made me uneasy.

Loading the horses and equipment onto the train was extremely hard. Eventually we did, so we started making our way towards Busan.

I don't remember how many days the journey took but we arrived safely at Busan. It took another day or two to load everything – horses, carriages, supplies – onto our transport ship, the *Tamatsumaru*. We set sail from Busan Port on the 9th of May.

The *Tamatsumaru* was a 10,000-tonne, high-speed vessel built specially for landing operations in Australia. It had special back doors for launching large landing boats, which made it valuable – and a major target. American submarines had bounties for sinking ships like this.

Despite its importance, the *Tamatsumaru* was travelling without any naval escort. And it was heading into Surigao Strait, one of the most dangerous waters in the area. It showed how desperate the war situation was.

We stopped briefly at Moji Port in Kyushu, Japan. That's when we finally learned our destination: Mindanao Island in the Philippines.

There were about 4,000 soldiers on board from all different parts of the army, plus we had horses, weapons, supplies and more. The soldiers overflowed into the corridors and onto the deck, leaving almost no space to put our feet down.

Since I was part of the field artillery unit, I had to help take care of the horses during the trip. The horses were kept in makeshift stables deep in the hold at the very bottom of the ship. Some of us made places to sleep by laying boards we'd found over the beams of the stable frame, while others had to rest on top of bags of feed, hay and supplies.

The heat was unimaginable. Plus, we also had to deal with the equally unimaginable smell of horse faeces that filled the air. I wasn't too distressed about that, however, because I was too busy praying we'd land safely in Mindanao. I was simply too nervous to think about anything else. None of us said it aloud but we'd all half given up on getting home alive. Still, I didn't want to die during the voyage and thought it would be better to have my life come to an end on the island of the battleground.

At night, we had to collect the horse faeces and pack them in straw bags with rocks to weigh the bags down. We then had to carry these bags all the way from the bottom of the ship, through the crowded hallways and out onto the deck so we could throw them into the sea.

We had to be very careful to ensure no horse waste ended up floating on the surface of the water. If it did, it could reveal our position to enemy submarines.

About a week after leaving Busan, there was an announcement. I thought it would be about arriving in the Philippines. Instead, we were told the fleet had to change course to avoid enemy submarines. We were now heading north into the East China Sea.

To reach the Port of Manila in Luzon, the fleet had to pass through the Bashi Channel – one of the most dangerous routes for submarine attacks. Looking back now, we were incredibly lucky to arrive safely.

Even though most days were filled with a mixture of nervousness and despair, we tried to find simple ways to pass the time. We helped the horses deal with the heat by giving them ice blocks we'd brought on board in Busan. We even made ourselves cold sugar water to drink. Sometimes, we gave the horses the *yokan* (sweet bean jelly) we'd secretly taken during the chaotic loading back in Busan.

Eventually, we were told we were approaching the Port of Manila.

17

Landing in the Philippines

On the 20th of May, just a few hours before we reached Manila, an aeroplane flew very low over our fleet. For a moment, we panicked, thinking it was an enemy air raid. But then we saw it – a red circle on the plane's wing. The symbol of Japan. A wave of relief swept through all of us.

We'd finally made it to Manila Bay. We were keen to get off the ship but this had to be done in shifts, with some soldiers staying behind to help with the horses and supplies. As I got ready to disembark, I realised something terrible – my boots were gone.

They'd been stolen just ten minutes before disembarkation.

Panic set in. I couldn't disembark barefoot. I had no choice but to steal another pair – and fast.

Boots are hard to replace because they come in different sizes. Mine were *11 mon 3 bu*, about 27.3 cm. Our boots had the size stamped into the heel – mine read 11:03.

Acting like nothing was wrong, I walked quickly around the ship, peeking into the messy areas where each company had their gear strung up on ropes. I couldn't find any boots in my size. Time was running out.

Then, near the Third Company's area, I saw them – a pair of boots marked 11:03, hanging near the corridor. I believed in the grace of heaven this time.

Quickly and quietly, I stole them. Then I ran for my life back to the stable, hoping no-one noticed. The boots were of good quality and probably belonged to an officer or a senior soldier. Inside the boots, I found a pair of slippers. The name on the label – Osugi – was one I recognised from my old company. The boots belonged to Sergeant Kiyoshi Osugi.

I had no choice, although I still felt guilty and was concerned about the incredible inconvenience my action would cause for Sergeant Osugi.

Finally, we were called to disembark. They'd set up a shower on land, so I grabbed a clean pair of underwear and headed to the deck. It had been a long time since I'd last showered. I went down the gangway and headed towards the place where the showers were located. Sergeant Osugi was standing right there. He was in perfect shape and was wearing a pair of great-looking boots. I was both shocked and relieved.

Inside a warehouse near the pier, there were tall stacks of filled brown sacks lining both sides of the walkway. Some of the sacks had spilled their contents, which had turned hard from being stepped on. A sweetness filled the air, so I pinched some that had spilled, putting it in my mouth as I walked past. Sugar! It was indeed granulated sugar.

I decided I wanted to take some back with me, so while I was showering I thoroughly washed the old pair of underwear I'd brought to use as a bag. On the way back, I filled the underwear-bag with sugar and continued onwards to the ship. We had ice for cooling down our horses, so I crushed some, poured in the sugar and made the most refreshing sweet ice water I'd ever tasted.

I don't remember how long we were anchored at the Port of Manila but once everyone had showered, we set sail again – this time heading for Cebu Island.

Along the way, our sister ship, *Kibitsumaru*, had engine trouble, so we made a quick stop at Iloilo, on Panay Island. Once the problem was fixed, we resumed our journey and finally reached Cebu – just across the strait from our final destination on Mindanao, Surigao.

Looking at the island brought feelings of hope. I even remember seeing the remains of an old pirate fort built into the stone behind a cove.

On the 25th of May, late in the afternoon, we reached Surigao. The first battalion had landed on Mindanao.

But now we had to get busy.

Some troops were headed south to different assignments, so we had to unload the horses, limbers, carriages and gear quickly. By the time we were ready to start unloading, it was pitch black. We split into two teams: one stayed on the ship, handing things down; the other used rope ladders to get off the side and receive everything.

The unloading dock was chaotic. It was so dark we couldn't tell who was who. Sometimes we grabbed gear or horses from other units by mistake, and they did the same to us.

We finished as dawn started to break. We could finally see where we were: a coastal town on a tropical island. Palm trees stood tall under a bright blue sky. Houses on stilts lined the shore.

And just like that, we'd officially arrived at the Southern Operations.

18

The Battle of Mindanao

In 1521, Ferdinand Magellan, a Portuguese explorer sailing for Spain, 'discovered' the Philippines. From that time, for almost 300 years, Spain controlled the islands.

In 1898, after the United States defeated Spain in the Spanish-American War, the Philippines became a colony of the United States. Unlike some other colonial powers, America treated its new colony differently. It focused on helping the economy grow, building schools and roads, and allowing free trade. Because of this, the Philippines was fairly peaceful and stable before Japan arrived, despite having been ruled by other countries for a long time. I first met the local people of the Philippines when I landed in Surigao, on Mindanao Island. Even though we'd arrived as an occupying army, they were surprisingly friendly and calm. Of course, they were probably used to life under foreign rulers, like Spain and America, so didn't show much fear.

One thing I heard many of them say, time and again, was: "General MacArthur said, 'I shall return' – so he definitely will. Please don't rampage all over the Philippines."

Those words stayed with me.

I'm not sure how many days we stayed in Surigao before marching south towards the east coast of Mindanao, our company's destination.

We had to be very alert because we'd been warned about guerrilla fighters still hiding in the area – especially those led by an American officer known as Lieutenant Marshall.

We were careful. The roads were decent and our draft horses were able to march without too much trouble. However, many of the bridges were destroyed so we had to take detours, going down into riverbeds and crossing rivers again and again.

Sometimes, though, we came across brand-new bridges, clearly built by the Japanese engineer units who'd arrived before us. However, these bridges were made for cars, not horses. They had spaced-out beams with thin wooden planks set where a car's tyres would go. For our four-horse teams, it was very tricky.

To cross safely, both the horses on the left had to walk on the left planks, and the horses on the right had to walk on the right ones. It was like walking across a sheet of ice, hoping the horses didn't lose their balance.

Then one evening – on our third or fourth day – it happened.

Just before reaching camp, as we were crossing a bridge, my right horse, Rensetsu, missed a step and its front leg fell between the wooden beams. When it happened, I was right at the front of the company with the first squad's limber.

Everything stopped. We quickly unhooked Rensetsu from the harness and, with help from the gunners, we pushed the limber by hand across the bridge.

We were shaking from nerves but we made it.

That night, we reached a small camp with an old American-style barracks in the middle of nowhere. It even had Western-style toilets, which were unfamiliar to us. But none of that mattered. All we could think about was Rensetsu's injured leg. We stayed up all night, taking turns to apply cold compresses, praying the leg would heal.

At that time, expecting that the American army would arrive by sea, the Japanese army's strategy was to defend the coast.

As soon as we arrived at Parang, a small village near a place named Cantilan, we started digging trenches and building positions along the shoreline. After finishing those, we moved into the jungles behind the coast to build gun positions on hills. There was, however, a big problem – there was no road to get the heavy limbers or gun carriages up there.

We had to make a road first.

It was tough work cutting through plants, breaking rocks and levelling the ground. Using just small shovels and pickaxes, we dug straight down, not checking how soft or hard the soil was.

One of the soldiers – an older man who used to work in civil engineering – warned us that the soil might collapse if we didn't build support beams as we dug. Sadly, he was right. On the third day, the hill suddenly gave way. Some of our team were buried in an instant.

It happened right after my group finished our shift. The next group had just started digging when the ground fell in. I heard a noise and by the time I'd turned around people were buried in the dirt. We rushed back to help dig them out. One of them was someone I'd joined up with – Sergeant Rokurou Matsui. He was buried almost up to the top of his head and it took a long time to get him out. He was in serious pain and was sent to the battalion's medical office. We never saw him again; although I heard a rumour later that he might have been sent home.

We were all frustrated. The company captain, a First Lieutenant from the military academy, was supposed to have planned everything out, but the way we'd been digging up the hill felt more like kids playing in a sandbox than a proper military operation. It was hard to trust his leadership after that.

After that incident, the plan to build positions on that hill was abandoned.

Afterwards, we just kept building more in the jungle, which brought its own set of problems. The jungle was thick with tropical plants and, as such, was hot, humid and filled with biting bugs – especially tiny black flies that swarmed our skin. We worked in our underwear, nothing else, and made bug candles from scrap cloth to create smoke to keep them away.

Despite everything, life settled into a routine. We started each day caring for the horses and exercising them. Other duties were rotated through: standing guard, stable duty, night shifts and fetching supplies and horse feed.

From time to time, local villagers would come to visit the nearby church. Early one morning, while I was on stable duty, I saw some villagers collecting *tubâ* – a kind of palm wine they'd set out to ferment the day before. I asked for a taste and they let me have some. It had been chilled by the night air and I still remember how cool and refreshing it was.

One day, we found out that part of the Third Company was going to pass near our village on their way to Tandag. We put together a delivery team to meet them. The team was led by Master Sergeant Shoukichi Nomoto, and I was the rear horse coachman on a four-horse carriage carrying supplies.

We travelled all day without any major trouble, delivered the packages and turned around to go back.

By then the sun had set so we decided to camp overnight. There were only five or six of us, with just our carriage, horses and small arms for defence. We found a vacant house to sleep in and took turns on guard duty. However, the villagers seemed nervous and we stayed alert all night. On the way back the next morning, we again noticed their odd behaviour. However, nothing happened and we made it back safely.

A few days later, I was promoted to Lance Corporal.

19

A Day Trip

Around this time, we began noticing American planes flying high above us. They flew alone or in groups and seemed to be watching our movements, but never attacked directly. Even so, every time we heard distant booming, we would all retreat into the jungle, just in case.

In early July, we received news that the island of Saipan had fallen. Not long after, the Tōjō Government in Japan stepped down, and a new Prime Minister, Kuniaki Koiso, took over.

At the end of July, I was ordered to accompany Master Sergeant Mouichi Yamada to the battalion headquarters in Tandag. To get there, we first travelled by foot to Surigao, where we boarded a small military boat called a *Daihatsu*, run by the ship engineering corps. The sea was calm and blue, the sky was clear and the warm ocean breeze reminded me of going to the beach as a child.

During the ride, one of the crew tied a wire hook to a bamboo fishing rod and tossed it into the water. Before long there was a definite bite. He caught a big bonito. He quickly cleaned it and served it raw as sashimi. We mixed powdered soy sauce with tea from our bottles and dipped the fish in this to eat. I hadn't eaten raw fish since joining the army and it tasted so good it almost made me cry.

We reached Tandag around midday. There, we were met by Master Sergeant Seiichi Fujisaki, someone I remembered from earlier days in Nanchang. While Master Sergeant Yamada was dealing with official business, I overheard Fujisaki telling him how terrible the war situation had become, and how unlikely it was that any of us would make it home alive.

That afternoon, we joined another marching unit and walked back to our company. As the sun began to set, we took a break in a forest of palm trees. Sergeant Yamada asked me to climb one of the tall trees and bring down some coconuts. I had to climb it in my boots, holding onto the rough trunk. As I was coming down, I lost my footing and slid all the way down, scraping both my bare arms. Once I hit the ground, blood was dripping down both arms and the pain was awful – but not as bad as when the medic poured iodine on the wounds. I couldn't help but to scream shamelessly.

20
Black Leopard Operation

The reason we'd been summoned to the headquarters was now clear: the loss of Saipan and Guam had changed everything. Japan could no longer rely on coastal defences alone.

Up until this point, our strategy had been to meet the enemy at the beach and stop them there. But now, from what we learned at Saipan, that strategy wouldn't work against the American forces.

A new plan was made – the Black Leopard Operation. Instead of waiting for the enemy on the coast, we'd first lead them inland. Then, we'd hide deep in the jungle, attack them by surprise and wipe them out.

The 30th Division were told that they would now act like leopards hiding in the jungle, waiting for the perfect moment to strike. We received something called 'The Pledge of the Leopard Corps', a fierce and dramatic statement about what we were being asked to do. It read:

We are the kings of the jungle, the black leopards of Mindanao.

We come from the divine nation of Japan from which wisdom shines.

We will bite the throats of the American devils and drink their raw blood.

We will surpass the limits of human strength by any means.

We give up all personal feelings and selfish desires.

We are 20,000 god leopards who will save the Empire.

We conquer the jungle, we sharpen our fangs, we polish our claws; in raging storms, in pitch-dark night, we will slaughter the American devils until they are destroyed.

The statement was meant to give us courage and prepare us mentally for what was coming. We were now part of a guerrilla-style battle, hiding in the jungle and striking when the enemy least expected it.

Around the same time, the horses we'd brought from North Korea began getting sick. They were used to freezing cold weather – able to handle temperatures as low as minus 20 degrees Celsius – but now we were near the equator. It was hot and humid. These horses just weren't built for this kind of climate and many of them started to suffer from illness.

The Japanese army had predicted that American forces would try to retake the Philippines, starting from the southern island of Mindanao, around early September. Because of this, the 30th Division was already getting into position on the northern coast of the island. After some early setbacks, we were told to move again – this time to the southern coast, around Davao.

My field artillery unit was sent to an area called Sarangani, at the very southern tip of Mindanao Island.

The plan was to first gather at Surigao, a port town at the northern end of the island. From there, we'd travel by boat to Cagayan, in central north Mindanao. Then we'd march across the island by land until we reached southernmost Sarangani.

It was the end of August when we began moving.

At that point, our group was split into two teams, or 'echelons'. The first echelon included gunners, spotters and communications operators. The second echelon, which I was assigned to, was mainly coachmen like me, responsible for transporting the horses.

The first echelon left Surigao on the 3rd of September and arrived in Cagayan on the 4th. My group, the second echelon, stayed behind and left on the 9th of September. Until then, we stayed busy taking care of the horses.

21
Tubâ Pitcher

The day before our departure, I was sent with a fellow soldier to buy some *tubâ* (local palm wine) for our group while they prepared for the dinner. Taking a large enamel pitcher-like container with us, we went into town.

At a small liquor shop, we tried to ask for *tubâ* using some broken Filipino and hand gestures. The women working there just looked confused. They didn't look like they were going to pour any *tubâ* into the container. We insisted more assertively and they suddenly all started laughing. Eventually, they looked at each other until one of them rolled up her skirt, straddled over our container and shouted, "Kore! Kore!" (This! This!) She was giggling hysterically and we finally realised what she was trying to communicate: the container we'd brought with us was actually a toilet bowl. We were so embarrassed but we laughed too.

Since we'd promised everyone some *tubâ*, we couldn't exactly go back empty-handed. We couldn't find any other suitable containers either, so we washed the toilet bowl as best we could and had the women fill it with *tubâ* anyway.

When we returned to the unit, dinner was ready and we gathered around with the others to drink a toast … but my fellow soldier and I declined.

22
Air Raid

Back at Surigao, the port was crowded. Warehouses were stacked with ammunition, food and other supplies, and many different-sized transport ships were waiting off the coast, anchored and ready to go.

Our group, the second echelon of the Second Company, assembled at the wharf early on the morning of the 9th of September. We loaded our horses efficiently, finishing around midday. I was just about to eat lunch on the deck when I was told by the anchorage headquarters to submit an embarkation list of names.

Reluctantly, I left the ship and returned to shore on a small rowboat. There, by the jetty, I sat in the hot sun, writing the names on lined carbon paper to make copies. I was sweaty, hungry and tired from a long morning of heavy work.

At approximately 1:30 pm, I noticed shadows sweeping across the ocean. I looked up and saw planes coming from the north-east, their engines roaring and explosions following close behind.

At first I thought the planes flying overhead were from our side – sent to protect us during the massive troop transfer. Then, without warning, they began diving down and bombing our sister ships waiting in the bay. Thick black smoke rose into the sky. Before any of us could fully comprehend what was happening, the enemy planes swooped in low and began dropping more bombs.

Explosions rocked the shore. The planes circled around and attacked again and again, ignoring all our rifle and machine-gun fire from the ground. Within a mere moment, the entire port had become a sea of fire.

I'd come to the port without any weapons – a few writing supplies was all I had with me.

As the attack raged on, I sprinted for cover towards the inland part of our camp, trying to dodge the bullets and explosions. The sand was hard to run on and every few steps I had to dive to the ground for cover as the enemy passed overhead. Soldiers were falling left and right around me, many of them screaming in pain. Or worse, not screaming at all.

I managed to run like hell and somehow escaped without being hit. I found shelter beneath a warehouse floor and caught my breath, only to realise I'd taken cover next to a pile of fuel drums and ammunition boxes – definitely not a safe place.

Quickly, I left and hid behind a big tree by the road. From there, I saw local villagers running around in fear and soldiers falling to the ground everywhere I looked. Some were groaning and some lay still with their guns held tightly in their arms, already gone.

Fires burned across the town. I even saw a charred pig crushed beneath a fallen palm tree.

Then I remembered something important – the list of names I'd been writing for the ship's log.

I'd left the embarkation list by the jetty!

It was not acceptable to leave it there, so I decided to go back for it despite the ongoing attack.

As I made my way to the jetty, I passed a group of horses tied up in a palm grove. They were panicking from the noise and smoke. A nearby officer shouted, "Which unit are you with?"

"Field artillery," I answered.

"Then free the horses!" he yelled.

I had no tools, so I asked to borrow his sword. With that, I cut the ropes and the horses ran off into the jungle.

Job done, I sprinted back to the jetty, dodging machine-gun fire and soldiers who'd fallen.

Somehow, I felt strangely calm – like the bullets wouldn't hit me. It was an odd, numb feeling but it gave me courage.

Miraculously, just ahead of me, I could see the embarkation list right where I'd left it, the white paper gleaming in the harsh afternoon sun as if it was just waiting for me to retrieve it.

I was so close – just one more step to reach it – but even that was still a frustrating distance. Finally, I stabbed the paper with the sword and turned to sprint back, still under successive machine-gun fire.

It wasn't until the sun was tending towards the west of the Bohol Sea, the bombing slowed. The sky quieted but the town of Surigao was reduced to ashes as far as the eye could see. Nevertheless, I made my way back to the beach, worried about the ship I'd been assigned to.

Dead and wounded soldiers were everywhere. One man walked towards me in a daze, his arm torn off and blood pouring from his shoulder. I was empty-handed and sadly there was nothing I could do. All the goods that had been previously piled around the wharf were also reduced to ashes and were still smouldering. The smell was pungent.

It was hell on earth. The scene in front of me is still burned into my mind, even now.

At the beach, I found a few others from the Second Company, including Hisazato Fukiya and Toshikazu Higashihara. They hadn't been on the ship either. From that day onwards, we stuck together.

Looking out at the water, I could see that most ships were still on fire or smouldering. Some had partially sunk, with only their stern sticking up out of the sea.

While we tried to figure out what to do next, we noticed people swimming to shore from the wrecked ships. Covered in black oil, they were heavily injured and many of them collapsed the moment they reached the beach. Some didn't survive.

Since nobody had proper clothes, we scavenged some items from nearby evacuated houses. Not long after the bombing stopped, we heard that the American forces might land at sunset. We weren't sure if it was true but we got ready just in case. We searched the beach and collected rifles, helmets, shoes and anything else we could find from fallen soldiers. We wanted to be prepared to fight, even with the little we had.

Later, we found out it was just a rumour – there was no landing that day. The air raids had also stopped. A few of us, including myself, took a small boat from the beach and rowed out to check the ships anchored offshore.

What we found was heartbreaking.

Everyone in Master Sergeant Tsuchie's unit had been killed in the attack. Most of the horses were dead too, and those that were still alive were in terrible condition. There was no way of rescuing them, so we shot them to put them out of their misery. We also counted the bodies we could find. It looked like some men had tried to escape by jumping into the ocean during the raid.

By the time we gathered the fallen soldiers' fingers[5] and the manes from the horses (for sending back as remains), the sun was already setting.

We returned to the beach on the small boat. The air was filled with embers and eerie thin streams of smoke rose to the sky.

Those of us who'd survived took shelter in a house at the base of a nearby mountain. We had no food, so we split into groups and went to search through the burned town, although we only found a few charred canned goods. We ate what we could and took turns

---

5. The fingers of fallen soldiers who were to be cremated were sent back to their families for consolation. However, as the war wore on, fewer families received the actual remains of their loved ones. Sometimes, families received white boxes containing nothing, or just containing bits of wood as symbols of bones.

keeping watch with weapons we'd taken from the dead.

23

The Morning After

The next morning, the sky was heavy and grey, as if it were about to rain – although these weren't any rain clouds. We left the beach early to walk through what was left of the town. It was in ruins as far as I could see.

The whole scene before me was like a message about the cruelty of war. Thin white plumes of smoke slowly rose into the sky, and a faint burning odour came from the piles of goods by the beach. At the water's edge, the surface of the ocean was so calm it was as if it, too, were dead. The horizon was foggy from the morning mist. The ocean surface and the sky blended in the same greyness. In the distance, the miserable wrecks of the transport ships were visible through the veil of dreary greyness.

We believed there might still be more survivors, so we searched the beach. Other units were also on the lookout for survivors and the beach became more and more crowded as time went by.

Two friends from my training days, Shinichi Nishino and Kouichi Iwamoto, somehow made it back. Kouichi's feet were injured and he couldn't walk, so Shinichi had found a cart and was pushing him along. They were wandering around aimlessly, dazed, when we encountered them.

The soldiers who'd swum to shore looked almost unrecognisable. The scant clothing they still wore was soaked in black oil. We gave them clothes we'd found in nearby houses and they took them gratefully. Some wore men's clothes, some women's – it was whatever we could find. We were a strange-looking group of soldiers at first, but after two or three days of gathering weapons and uniforms from fallen soldiers, we began to look like a proper army again.

Then came more bad news. The first echelon, who'd arrived at Cagayan ahead of us, had also been heavily bombed around the same time we were attacked in Surigao.

After three or four days of chaos, we managed to regroup. Once we had clear leadership again, we were given new orders. We were to march overland to a small port town called Nasipit. From there, we would take a ship to Cagayan and continue our mission.

24
Surigao to Cagayan

The road between Surigao and Nasipit was dangerous. Guerilla fighters were active in the area, led by an American officer named Captain Marshall who had stayed behind in Mindanao to continue fighting. Many local people supported the guerillas, as the anti-Japanese sentiment among the local residents was strong. The rough, mountainous terrain also made it easier for them to operate.

We eventually managed to join the other units heading to Nasipit. We had no artillery, vehicles, or draft horses left – just a few carts and wagons we'd found in the chaos. We loaded all our remaining supplies on them to be pulled by small local horses. The march of these tired horses and weary soldiers was slow and disheartening.

The road was like a narrow country road in the Japanese mountains, with low hills on both sides and small streams crossing it. Drinking fresh water was forbidden, and we always made sure to boil water before using it. But one day, we saw small fish floating belly-up in a nearby stream. The guerillas had poisoned the water from upstream. Boiling it wouldn't help – we were left without any safe water.

Many of the bridges across the winding rivers had been destroyed. The advance teams had dug out paths down to the riverbeds so we could cross, although it was hard going. As we marched, the signs of guerilla activity increased but we were not directly attacked. Eventually, we reached the small port town of Nasipit.

From Nasipit, we boarded steam schooners – ships brought from Japan and run by the army's ship engineers. The crews were made up of boys who were four or five years younger than me. By then, we'd lost track of the calendar, but I believe it was near the end of September.

Since the air raid on Surigao on the 9th of September, we'd become terrified of aeroplanes. After our schooner left the dock at Nasipit and moved offshore, we heard explosions again in the distance. Panicked, we moved the ship close to the coast and hid behind palm trees until it was safe. Once the sound faded, we returned to our route. It was a voyage filled with trepidation. Landing safely at Cagayan, it felt like we'd escaped a tiger's jaws.

We stayed in Cagayan for two or three days. It was decided that we'd continue across Mindanao to reach Sarangani. While waiting, I visited some soldiers who'd been hospitalised after the bombing of Cagayan on the 9th of September. Sadly, many never recovered enough to return home. Some died from illness, others died in later battles. And some had taken their own lives when the enemy arrived.

25
Cagayan to Malaybalay

We left Cagayan to transport newly received supplies to Sarangani.

The Philippines lies near the equator, with dry and wet seasons. As we travelled from northern Mindanao to the southern region of Sarangani, we found ourselves in the thick of the wet season. South of Malaybalay, we were told the roads were in such bad condition that it was impossible to plan our route with any certainty.

The first echelon, ahead of us, had tried to transport limbers but were stuck in hip-deep mud, barely able to move more than a few dozen metres each day. On top of that, they were attacked by locals and lost several men.

Up to Malaybalay, we made decent progress along the national road. Still, American planes attacked frequently with machine-gun fire, forcing us to scatter and take cover again and again.

Soon after leaving Cagayan, we passed through Del Monte. The fields there were full of pineapples, though most had already been eaten by the units before us. We kept walking deeper into the fields until we finally found some ripe ones. The sweet and sour, fully ripe, warm pineapples grown under the tropical sun were unbelievably delicious.

Even during these brief moments of joy, American planes continued to strafe us with gunfire, so we always had to be vigilant. We reached a small stretch of hilly land and followed the road that cut through sloping fields towards our next destination, Maluko.

Finding ripe pineapples in the pineapple field.

Bright green grasslands stretched far in every direction, dotted with trees. It felt so peaceful that I wanted to throw myself on the carpet of the green grass and forget all about the reality of war for a while. I thought, *if only these American planes would leave us alone*. That image played in my mind as we marched on through this tranquillity.

Then we spotted the shadow of a plane overhead. Explosions followed. We braced for an attack. The commander, First Lieutenant Sami, used his proud possession – high magnification binoculars – and confidently shouted, "Friendly forces!"

We relaxed.

A moment later, the plane swooped down and opened fire. Chaos erupted. We had no cover in the open fields. I jumped into a roadside stream and hid under a small earthen bridge.

Incidents like that happened almost daily. Still, we made it to Malaybalay safely after several nights and without major losses.

Malaybalay was one of the largest cities in Mindanao, after Davao. It had once been a major base for American and Filipino troops before Japan invaded. When we arrived, both the division and regiment headquarters were there. On the surface, the townspeople seemed cooperative, and there were sufficient supplies of food, clothing and other necessities.

We were scheduled to rest there for three days before continuing south towards Sarangani. The path would take us through Kibawe, Omonay, Kabacan, Dulawan, Koronadal and Tupi.

A few days after we left Malaybalay, we arrived at a small village. It was a bright, sunny day, so while everyone rested, I finally washed my clothes – a rare luxury. Our company leader, Second Lieutenant Yamaoka, suggested we each compose a haiku during the short break. The theme was the air raid on the 9th of September.

I improvised:

Ano tomo mo (Our dear comrades and)

Umamo kaerazu (Our kind horses, return not)

Akinoumi (From the autumn sea)

This was the heartache of the battlefield, where I stood caked in sweat and mud.

26

Marching Through Mud

The road conditions between Kibawe, Omonay, Kabacan and Dulawan were especially terrible. The road was worse than we'd imagined and was a continuous quagmire as we made our way through the height of the rainy season. Hip-deep mud in places meant we sometimes only moved a few dozen metres a day. It reminded me of the lotus fields outside Osaka, near my hometown. Calling it a 'road' was way too generous.

Malaria-carrying mosquitoes attacked us constantly, sapping our energy. We'd brought mosquito nets but they wore out quickly from constant use and, even though we kept repairing them, hygiene became difficult to maintain. Many soldiers developed fevers and diarrhoea. Despite our precautions, sickness spread and the march slowed.

Since leaving Malaybalay, we'd received no new supplies. We had to rely completely on what we could take from local people. Shoes and rubber-soled socks wore out quickly in the muddy marches. We patched what we could and scavenged the rest.

At one point, I made a pair of *geta* (wooden sandals) out of scrap wood and rope. They reminded me of home. A fellow soldier from a farming village taught me how to make *zori* (straw sandals), which were better suited for the rain or on muddy roads. I made use of this *zori*-making technique until the very end of the war.

Many soldiers got sick from the harsh conditions. Our medics had no medicine. Some of us tried strange remedies, like eating blackened charred potato skins to treat diarrhoea. I stayed relatively healthy, but I remember one bad case of constipation. I suffered for days. Somehow, following someone's suggestion

– drinking a mess tin full of heavily salted water – turned out to be the cure.

Toothaches were another problem. I once tried to pull out a molar with horse-shoeing pliers borrowed from a farrier. I failed. Instead, I packed coal tar in the cavity. It dulled the pain but didn't stop it.

Time became meaningless. Days and nights blurred together as we slogged through 400 kilometres of jungle and mud through Mindanao Island, dreams and reality intertwined. All I could think about was that I just wanted to arrive at Sarangani and face my next fate.

In one place, we came across the remains of a shed. Guerrillas had attacked sick soldiers resting there. Among the dead were my old roommate from the Pyongyang hospital, Shizuo Ihara, and two classmates, Masao Ando and Kouji Juuichiya.

The rain, malaria, guerrilla attacks and endless mud took their toll. Many soldiers collapsed and couldn't go on. 'Field hospitals' were set up here and there, but they were really just shacks where these 'dropout' soldiers were left behind. The abandoned dropout soldiers never returned to the main body. Most died there of sickness. Some who survived died later in battle or by suicide.

27
At Sarangani

We arrived at Sarangani around mid-November, having somehow endured the long and brutal march. There, we supplied artillery equipment to the second and third battalions. They'd lost many of their guns and carriages in earlier American air raids at Sarangani and Surigao.

I'd lost track of time by that point – except for the date of the 9th of September air raid at Surigao. But I clearly remember one serene, moonlit night in Sarangani. We welcomed the New Year with salt-grilled catfish, caught in the stream beside the palm grove where the horses were tethered.

By then, the activities of American planes had become noticeably more frequent. Planes flew over daily, launching small strafing and bombing attacks. It felt like they were probing us, trying to trigger a response and gauge our strength.

Sarangani faced a vast bay. Near the coast, the remnants of a cotton field spread out, with a narrow airstrip along one edge and grassy meadows behind it. A river curved around the meadow and jungle stretched beyond it, leading into the hills.

Our Second Company was camped in this jungle. A few kilometres farther in was the site of a former village where the Navy Construction Party had set up camp—we called it 'Navy Hamlet'. Another few kilometres beyond that was our battalion headquarters.

Almost every day, American planes flew high overhead – either solo or in small formations. They passed far above, heading north, while our own aircraft never appeared.

Our camp was set up at the jungle's edge. In the centre of the camp stood a giant camphor-like tree.

Around it, squads built shacks and lived under its canopy. The tree bore bright red fruit[6], bean-sized when seen from below, yet when they fell you could see they were actually similar in size to *umeboshi* (Japanese pickled plum).

Monkeys were the most memorable of the many creatures that shared the jungle with us. Every five to seven days, they came to eat the red fruit. At first, they were cautious and stayed only briefly; we just watched them from a distance.

Eventually, both sides grew used to each other. The monkeys lingered longer. Coincidentally, around this same time, we ran out of food. We decided to shoot a monkey to eat.

One day, we waited beneath the tree, taking aim. From below, they looked only a little larger than Japanese monkeys, but it was only when we

---

6. The type of tree was not written; however, it was possibly the Bignay tree (*Antidesma bunius*) or a type of fig.

approached one that had fallen that we realised how big they really were. We hesitated, but shouldn't have as the rest of the troop began throwing fruit and faeces down at us.

This spurred us into action and we fired a shot, causing them to flee – at first. They soon returned to rescue their fallen friend. We watched as the one wounded monkey clung to a branch and was pulled up by the others. Then, supporting it from branch to branch, together they carried it away.

It shocked me. I was unnerved by how the monkeys resisted our attempt to capture their member – and how they worked together to save the injured.

Looking back, it reminded me painfully of our own retreat. We had left behind our sick and wounded friends during the march. These monkeys, on the other hand, had done everything to save their own.

28
Navy Hamlet

One day, I was given orders to join the navy construction team in a small village we called the 'Navy Hamlet'.

My job there was to help build a simple workshop in the jungle and make backpack-style depth charges, which were small bombs carried like backpacks. We were preparing in case enemy tanks landed.

There were about fifteen or sixteen people in the group. Ten were from the navy; the rest were infantrymen and others like me. Because I had the highest rank among the army group, I became the supervisor.

The army soldiers were split into pairs or small groups and joined different teams in the navy construction team. We lived together and even got paid for our work.

Most of the navy team – except for the officers – were older men who had been drafted. Like us, they had left their families behind to serve in the war. Some were old enough to have daughters in high school.

They were skilled craftsmen like carpenters, plasterers, blacksmiths and cabinetmakers. They hadn't received proper military training and didn't even know how to take apart or clean a rifle. But they were kind to us young army soldiers and always called us 'Riku-san, Riku-san' (which means 'Mr Land').

Every morning, we gathered for a roll call in front of the officer's quarters before training began. For us army soldiers, the exercises were optional. Navy drills had a different rhythm and style from ours, and we couldn't keep up with them very well. We also didn't have to do daily chores, so life there was easier than usual. But even then, we couldn't forget that we were still in the middle of a war. Every day, we listened to the news on the radio outside the officers' quarters.

Our main job was to build an ignition device for fighting enemy tanks. We cut small wooden blocks and drilled holes in them. Into each hole, we placed a used musket shell without the gunpowder. Then we added a fuse and a safety pin made of wire. The fuse was attached to a small wooden box packed with explosives. The box was about the size of a fruit crate. We tied it up with rope so it could be carried like a backpack.

To use it, a soldier would sneak up to a tank, pull the safety pin, strike the igniter to start the fuse and throw himself under the tank to blow it up. Basically, it was for suicide bombing.

For about a month, I worked with the navy craftsmen and saw just how talented they were. Once, they made a Japanese sword out of scraps they found.

First, a mechanic salvaged leaf springs from abandoned vehicles.

A charcoal maker – who'd learned his craft in the mountains back home – handled the tempering. He built a furnace deep in the jungle, carefully selecting suitable wood, cutting it down and turning it into charcoal. During the day, he loaded the furnace, lit the fire at sunset and adjusted the chimney vent. He retrieved the charcoal the following morning. A single miscalculation in adjusting the airflow – combined with unpredictable weather – could result in complete failure, reducing everything to ashes or leaving the wood unburned.

A blacksmith used this charcoal to heat the metal, adjusting the temperature with a pair of bellows. Two smiths took turns hammering the glowing steel, shaping it into a *katana* (a traditional Japanese sword with a long blade).

A grinder then spent days honing the edge, and a cabinetmaker intricately crafted a wooden scabbard and handle. Finally, the 'Japanese sword' was complete – a truly brilliant piece of craftsmanship.

Beyond sword-making, the craftsmen also taught me how to create other practical tools for daily survival.

My time with the navy construction team lasted only a month but during my stay I was fortunate to receive treatment for a persistent toothache from a combat medic who specialised in dentistry.

The treatment, however, was nothing like what I would have received from a dentist back home. The field equipment was rough, and there was no electricity, so I had to pedal with my feet to power the grinding drill. The pain was excruciating and, with a limited supply of anaesthetics, I broke into a cold sweat during the procedure. Still, once it was over, I felt a huge sense of relief. I was truly thankful. If I hadn't joined this team, I probably would've had to live with that pain much longer.

After we finished our assigned work, I returned to my original unit. Even though I hadn't been with the navy group for long, I'd made strong friendships with some of the navy soldiers. Later, when the Americans attacked and we had to escape into the jungle, those very same friends helped me survive. Without their kindness, I might not have made it home.

Food was very hard to find. Most days, we went to a burned field to search for leftover potatoes that hadn't been dug up. One day, we found a wild hog in the jungle. We managed to kill it, then brought it back and ate until we were full. That was such a rare treat.

After the meal, we buried the hog's bones in a deep hole. The next morning, we found a large lizard had fallen in. We cooked and ate that too. Lizards may look scary but they actually tasted fine. At that point, I ate whatever I could find and because of that, I stayed fairly healthy compared to some of the others.

Many soldiers were growing weak from hunger. We couldn't find enough food ourselves anymore, so the company planned a large food-gathering mission. I'd also been feeling unwell and was resting in the 'recovery room' near our camp, when a fellow soldier, Lance Corporal Kadowaki, came to me. "I'm sorry to disturb you while you're resting," he said, "but we've run out of food. Do you think you could join the food run?"

I felt like I'd recovered enough, so I agreed to go.

29

Surprise Bombing

The next morning, we left with two wagons pulled by horses, led by Master Sergeant Yamada. As we walked across a wide open field, we saw a group of large planes in the sky. A split second later, we heard the roaring of furious explosions. We quickly hid under a tall tree. Overhead were five or six big bombers with fighter planes flying around them.

In the blink of an eye, they roared past towards the jungle and unleashed a relentless bombing attack. The deafening sound of explosions echoed through the air. Anxiously, we watched the direction of the attack, fearing that our Navy Hamlet had been targeted.

We reassured ourselves that it couldn't have been and, once the bombing stopped, we resumed our mission to collect food from the village.

There was little resistance from the villagers and we managed to secure more food than we'd hoped for.

That evening, as the sun was setting, we prepared dinner over a bonfire by the riverbed. Then, two soldiers on horseback rode up fast. One was Sergeant Ozaki. They brought grave news that our camp had been bombed and many soldiers were dead. We were ordered to return immediately. Without hesitation, we made our way back through the dark night.

The devastation at the company was overwhelming. The 'recovery room', where I'd just been staying, had taken a direct hit. Everyone inside had died instantly. The realisation hit – I'd only survived because I'd gone on the food run.

Some of the people who died were friends who had slept beside me every night. I heard horrifying stories about how they died.

Master Sergeant Nomoto had been torn apart, his limbs scattered all over the area. Motoh Kawakita was found dead without any visible injuries, likely killed by the shockwave of the blast. Kesae Shinohara had suffered a severe abdominal wound. He lay dying, shouting, "Long live the Emperor," while desperately trying to push his intestines back into his body, before passing away.

After keeping the fingers as remains, we set about burying the bodies. However, with the tree roots forming a tangled net just beneath the surface, it was impossible to dig deep graves. We could only dig shallow pits, place the bodies inside, cover them with soil and build small grave mounds with wooden posts as markers.

With so many comrades gone, there were fewer of us left to share the work and I was soon assigned to stable duty.

The stable was located right next to the burial ground where my comrades, who'd been alive and beside me just days before, now lay in their shallow graves. The horse well was on the far side of the graves and the flickering glow of the kindling coals cast eerie shadows over the crude wooden grave posts. Every now and then, wildcats or some other nocturnal creatures let out strange cries in the darkness. Fear gripped me and the night felt unbearably long as I waited for the next soldier to relieve me.

Our camp was built around a huge tree, and we were constantly cleaning the surrounding area to keep it tidy. Unfortunately, that clear space made us easy to spot from the sky. Looking back, it may have been safer if we'd covered the area with branches and leaves.

A few days after the bombing, the Master Sergeant asked me to help deliver the remains of soldiers who'd died since the attacks on Surigao and Cagayan. We were to take them from battalion headquarters to the regimental headquarters in Malaybalay. I was reluctant. I said I still wasn't feeling well. The sergeant wasn't happy with my excuse; however, he arranged to send Lance Corporal Kyoji Kawasaki from Kamiichi, Nara, instead.

On the day he left for battalion headquarters, I ran into him in a palm grove. We talked for a moment and wished each other the best of luck. "There should be more supplies in Malaybalay than here in Sarangani," I said. "You might need money. I don't need it, so please take mine." I gave him everything I had.

In April, I heard that American forces had landed at Cotabato, and then stormed into Malaybalay, where our army's leaders were. By June, our regimental leaders were running out of options and decided to escape. They went down the Umayan River in rafts and were never seen again. It's believed they fell into a huge waterfall basin that even the locals avoided.

I often wonder if Lance Corporal Kawasaki was among them, carrying my money – and my fate – with him.

30

Battle Preparation

On the 31st of December, our division ordered the 74th Infantry Regiment to move to Malaybalay.

As the New Year began, the enemy's attacks grew stronger. On the 24th of March, we were told to withdraw from Sarangani, head back to Davao and then rejoin our unit in Malaybalay. We left Sarangani on the 26th of March.

We marched through several towns – Polomolok, Tupi, Marbel, and Tacurong – before arriving in Lambayong on the 6th of April. As we passed through Sapakan, we suddenly heard loud explosions coming from the direction of Cotabato. Thick black smoke filled the sky. Soon after, we received a radio message confirming that American forces had landed in Cotabato and were moving east along the Pulangi River.

Due to this unexpected turn of events, we couldn't continue to Malaybalay. New orders arrived: we had to turn around and defend Sarangani instead. We returned on the 14th of May.

When we got back, we started building defences every day in preparation for the enemy's landing, which we anticipated in the near future. We worked on 'Heigei Mountain[7]', a rocky hill with a view of Sarangani Bay. Our job was to make a cave for an observation post and gun position by digging straight into the rock.

We camped in a shack near a river at the base of the mountain. Each morning, we packed two bananas or corn for lunch, took two ammunitions and headed to the mountain. We stored the ammunition in a

---

7. Not its actual name. *Heigei* means 'to glare' or 'look down on' in Japanese.

trench, then chipped at the rock using just chisels and hammers. The rock was harder than we expected.

When cracks formed in the rock, we packed the holes with small explosives and lit a fuse. Then we ran to take cover. Each blast removed a small chunk of rock. After several days, we'd made a cave big enough for two people. We kept digging and, as we went deeper, had to carry out the blasted rock and throw it down the hill. Eventually, American planes noticed the piles of rubble.

Each time a plane flew by, we had to stop working and hide. Sometimes, the fuse was already lit when a plane came, and we had to dive for cover. But finally, on the 9th of July, the cave was completed.

That evening, we finished work early and gathered by the river. Each squad cooked dinner and we celebrated finishing the cave. I sang a song from 1940 called *Aiba Hanayome* and made sweets called *kintsuba* using pumpkin paste. Everyone clapped, savouring a long-forgotten atmosphere of joy.

Suddenly, we heard a strange noise. A flare lit up the sky, illuminating the entire area as if it were midday. We quickly hid in the jungle. Once darkness returned, we wondered what the enemy had planned next.

The next morning, we climbed back up to Heigei Mountain to observe the sea. Countless ships filled Sarangani Bay, but there was no sign of a landing yet. Enemy patrol planes flew overhead again and again.

That night, without warning, the enemy began a terrifying bombardment from their ships. The sound of their guns was unlike anything I'd ever heard – a force so atrocious it felt as though it shook the entire earth. First came the faraway booming of the gun being fired. A few seconds later came the crash of the shell landing near us. If the next explosion was farther away, we were relieved. But if it was closer, our fear grew because we knew the next one might hit us. Each moment was full of dread as we waited for the next explosion.

When the barrage finally passed beyond our area, we knew we were safe – for now.

31
Landing of the American Forces

Early on the morning of the 12th, the enemy arrived with a huge number of ships full of soldiers, weapons and tanks. They landed quickly and started to build up their base near the beach. Tanks rolled in first, followed by artillery and many more troops.

Our guns were on high ground near the Klinan River. As soon as the enemy reached the river, we fired on them. It was a surprise attack and seemed to cause a lot of confusion, but soon, their scout planes flew overhead and we were spotted. Their fighter planes began shooting at us and their cannons fired back with great power. They had many more supplies than we did. Every time we fired, they fired back ten times more.

That night, our soldiers, along with some navy troops, launched surprise attacks. We inflicted considerable damage but the enemy fought back hard. Every thirty minutes, their cannons fired at us for thirty minutes. They kept pushing forward.

As the enemy steadily advanced, we tried our best to slow them but we soon ran out of shells for our cannons. We had no choice but to take apart the guns, destroy the parts and push them down the gorge below.

Under the cover of darkness, we retreated into the jungle of Mount Magolo.

During the cannon fight, I was at the observation post with our commander. Just as we fired our final shot, an enemy shell landed between us and the battery position, as if perfectly timed. It destroyed our communication lines.

We followed the previously agreed plan: destroy the guns and run. Each of us retreated after disposing of everything except for the emergency supply of '1.8

litres of rice, salt, a tent, a rifle, bullets', plus a field phone.

32

Roaming in the Jungle

We headed into the jungle of Mount Magolo. Enemy planes were flying overhead all the time, so we couldn't move during the day. Even moving at night was difficult. To prevent the planes from seeing the fire and smoke, we could only cook food and boil water quickly at dawn or dusk.

Before long, we'd run out of rice and had to search for food. Unfortunately, the jungle had very little to offer. Some people were so hungry they ate anything they could find – even if it made them sick.

In the evening, we searched abandoned farms for leftover potatoes or corn. We also picked wild plants. We'd boil everything together in our mess kits. We'd run out of salt and had no other seasonings so none of it tasted good but it helped fill our stomachs.

Lack of salt was a big problem. Our bodies craved it so badly we even resorted to licking the sweat off our friends' backs to try and get a little salt intake. One day, while looking at the sea in the distance, I dreamed of running down to the shore, drinking seawater until I was full and then dying. The thought didn't worry me as I felt I wouldn't survive for much longer anyway.

Some of my friends were severely malnourished and couldn't walk anymore because their legs were so swollen. Each day, they grew weaker and weaker. We'd lean on each other as we moved. The sight of us stumbling through the jungle, barely holding each other up, must have looked like a scene from hell.

We walked at night, using only the moonlight to guide us. One time, we reached a cliff covered in vines. We climbed down using the vines like ropes, our feet finding small notches in the rock. I was the first one down. Just as I turned to help the others, some people jumped out of the bushes ahead of us, shouting words I didn't understand. It sounded like "Shui ya!" I thought they were Chinese soldiers and shouted, "Fire! Fire!" But no-one fired.

The people shouted back, "Japanese army! Friendly forces!" Then they said loudly, "Shinshu! Shinshu! Shinshu!"

Shinshu (Land of Gods) was the password we'd all learned, and I realised then that they were Japanese. I quickly yelled, "Don't shoot! They're friendly!"

A Japanese officer stepped forward. "Who shouted just now?" he asked.

Luckily, someone else smoothed things over and we all moved on. I was embarrassed. I'd forgotten the password and almost caused a deadly mistake.

Even though we had close calls like that, we managed to stay together in a somewhat orderly manner. We still had the strength to consider the ones who were unwell. When someone got sick, we stopped to build a small camp to rest, searched for food and used the time to figure out our next move.

But the enemy never stopped.

Their planes kept searching for us. If they saw even the slightest sign of the Japanese army, they opened fire or dropped bombs. Artillery from the ground also reached us sometimes.

More of our soldiers were hurt by bullets and bombs. Some developed bad infections with their wounds filling with pus. They grew too weak to walk and although we tried to help them by making walking sticks or carrying their gear, our own strength was also fading. We barely had enough energy to keep moving ourselves, let alone carry another person.

Sometimes, we had to leave people behind. We told them, "Rest here. Once we make a camp, we'll come back to get you." But often, they were already dead by the time we returned. Their bodies would be laying lifeless, giant ants swarming in and out of their ears, noses and mouths.

The jungle had become a graveyard. We were just trying not to join the dead.

33
Mount Magolo

Mount Magolo (1,487 m) was constantly shrouded in clouds. It was a dangerous place, and home to the Moro people, a group of strong-willed Muslim villagers. Despite the risks, we had no choice but to head there as it was said to have deposits of rock salt.

We pressed on through the jungle, retreating deeper and deeper to escape the relentless pursuit of American forces. Halfway up Mount Magolo, across a small river, we found a cave. The entrance was about ten metres wide but it was much bigger inside. It was a limestone cave and went deep into the mountain. This cave became a temporary refuge for us – about 1,000 army and navy soldiers who'd fled into the jungle.

It looked like bandits had used the cave before because there were old fire pits – not that these were of any use to us as we had no food. We were existing on water retrieved from the stream at night. Many of our men were suffering from malaria or were weak from severe malnourishment. We had nowhere else to go, so we stayed there for three or four nights.

On the second day, American scouts must have spotted our cave. A few enemy soldiers came near and fired their guns randomly, perhaps hoping we'd shoot back and give away our position. We didn't, though. We were too weak to fight and just stayed quiet, waiting for their withdrawal. Over the course of the three-day standoff, some soldiers died and some others' illnesses became worse. According to our lookout, enemy activity was increasing. Sensing the urgency, our leader ordered us to brace ourselves for a desperate last stand – a suicidal counterattack. Then, just when we were preparing for one final battle, the lookout returned with surprising news. The enemy had left.

After the sun set, some of us went for a patrol to confirm the enemy had definitely withdrawn. We found a shallow hole and some cans of peas and carrots where the enemy had been. They must have been keeping watch but decided to pull back. We brought the cans back to the cave, opened them with our swords and devoured every last morsel, including the brine. They tasted incredible – so much so that I can still recall the sensation on my tongue and throat to this day.

The next evening, as twilight approached, we emerged from the cave, preparing to retreat further into the mountains. However, the days spent hiding had taken a heavy toll. The ill soldiers had become even weaker and even those who'd been relatively healthy were now showing symptoms of fever and beriberi. By the time we were ready to move, the number of sick and weakened men had nearly doubled since we'd first arrived.

We faced a painful dilemma: what to do with the dead. The mountain was rocky, making it impossible to bury them. Cremation was out of the question – any smoke or fire would risk revealing our position to the enemy. Instead, we gathered branches and leaves, just enough to cover the bodies.

Then there was also the question of who we could take with us. Those who could still walk left under the cover of night. As for the ill soldiers, we assured them that we'd return for them once we'd established a new base.

In the pitch-black jungle without the moonlight, we navigated an unfamiliar and treacherous landscape by following a narrow stream. Those in front led the way for the weak and malnourished, some of whom had lost their glasses, while others were suffering from night blindness due to malnutrition. They had to be guided with sticks. Even so, some lost their footing and slipped down the rocky gorge.

Just as the sky began to lighten, and after what felt like countless kilometres, we finally arrived at the remnants of a Moro village on a gentle mountain slope. We decided to build a temporary shelter in the nearby forest to establish a base.

Constructing a jungle shelter followed a familiar pattern: we selected a sturdy tree as a central pillar, cut down surrounding trees and laid timber beams to form the roof and floor. Rafters and joists were spaced as needed, then covered with layers of jungle foliage to provide shelter from the rain and protection from ground-dwelling pests. We had no nails or tools – only the crude knives we'd taken from the local village – we bound the structure together using raw jungle vines.

However, the jungle leaves dried and shrunk almost immediately, and the daily storms quickly soaked us. Each time it rained, we had to reinforce and repair the shelter.

Four or five days after we finished building the shed and had managed to gather a small amount of food by digging through the remains of burned fields, we became concerned about the sick and injured soldiers we'd left behind. A few of us decided to retrace our steps back to the cave.

As we followed the creek downstream, we came across several bodies – men who'd pushed themselves to their limits, desperately trying to keep up with us despite their deteriorating condition, only to collapse and take their final drink from the stream before dying.

The relentless heat and daily storms made their bodies rot quickly and wild hogs had scavenged on them, making it hard to tell who they were.

34
Back at the Cave

When we finally made it back to the cave, we were met with a heartbreaking scene. Bodies were lying all around – soldiers who'd died after we left. Only five men were still alive and conscious. They looked very weak, but their eyes were open and alert. Scattered around them were empty boxes of military food, American medicine bags and small glass ampules with English writing on them.

The sick soldiers told us that not long after we'd left, a group of American soldiers came to the cave. Among them was a combat medic and a soldier who seemed to be Japanese-American. He acted as their interpreter.

The Americans had asked them some questions, checked their health and then given them medicine, injections and food.

The interpreter told them:

"Your Japanese comrades abandoned you and fled deeper into the jungle. America is your true friend now. We can't move you yet, but we'll come back with more food and medicine. When you're strong enough, we'll take you to an American hospital. Stay strong and don't lose hope."

The Americans had returned daily, bringing food and medicine.

Starved from our constant struggle in the jungle, we ate the ill soldiers' leftovers. As the next American visit drew near, they urged us to leave: *"The Americans will be here soon. Please leave now. We believe what they told us. We'll stay and surrender to Americans."*

We tried to persuade the sick soldiers to come with us but they refused. They believed the Americans would return to help them. So, with no other choice, we left the cave and went back to our shelter.

A few days later, we returned to the cave to check on them – it was completely empty except for some empty food boxes, medicine containers and small glass ampule. The soldiers were gone. Our only conclusion was that the Americans must have come back and taken them away. I stood there for a while, flabbergasted. If things had been the other way around, would we, Japanese soldiers, have treated the enemy with the same kindness?

This wasn't just about having more supplies. It felt like something deeper – a difference in how people were raised. Maybe it had to do with the way American soldiers were taught about helping others from a young age. I didn't know if it was the religious influence, such as Christianity, but it seemed like their actions came from something they'd believed in from an early age. A sense of humanitarianism, perhaps.

35
Survival in the Jungle

The enemy's aircraft remained relentless, sweeping the valleys and searching for any signs of us. When they spotted something, they'd open fire or drop bombs without warning. Sometimes, ground artillery would also start shooting at us again, as if to remind us they hadn't forgotten we were still there.

In our jungle shelter, I continued my daily struggle for survival. Each day, I wandered through the forest, looking for anything I could eat. I stumbled upon an already-harvested potato field one day, while wandering aimlessly with my sword. Scavenging through it, I found only scraps – tiny, leftover potatoes, like a mouse's hidden stash.

I was barely able to keep my hunger at bay. Meanwhile, malnutrition and malaria claimed my friends one by one on a daily basis. The names of those who passed blur in my memory. I can no longer recall who was the first to go and who followed, but among them were Taisuke Konno, Shigeru Yamashita, Akira Kanda, Sakunojo Iwamoto, Akira Uchida and Isamu Higashiura.

Around the same time, I started feeling feverish, probably from malaria. I rested in the shelter for about three days, but with no food left, I knew I had to eat or I'd only get weaker. I forced myself to get up. Holding a bayonet in one hand and my mess kit – now missing its lid – in the other, I tried to walk, but my legs were weak from lying down for so long. I couldn't even cross a narrow log bridge and had to crawl over it instead.

I gathered whatever I could find – sweet potato vines, wild leaves – and brought them back. I boiled everything in the mess kit, mixing it with the remains of my last meal that was stuck to the bottom. The result was an unidentifiable, bitter stew – but I ate it all. Wasting food wasn't an option. If I had stayed lying down, I would have died from starvation and illness. My friends would have had no choice but to bury me in the soil.

Each day, foraging for food became our only task. Soldiers, acting on their own, wandered the jungle like lost souls. Our unit had fallen apart. There was no order, no command. We had become nothing more than a desperate, starving mass of scattered survivors.

In early August, American planes began dropping leaflets, telling us to surrender. At first, we thought it was just a trick. But soon the leaflets showed photos of Japanese prisoners in American camps. They looked well-fed and at ease. The leaflets also showed the suffering of people back in Japan and the destruction caused by the war. For those of us who'd already lost the will to fight, these images planted the seeds of doubt.

Around this time, we noticed something strange – enemy planes were flying overhead without opening fire and bombing from the ground artillery had stopped. A change was in the air.

Then, on the 25th of August, a radio at the battalion headquarters that was, at the time, undergoing repairs, suddenly picked up a transmission: Japan had surrendered on the 15th of August. We immediately checked this news with other nearby units.

It was confirmed. The war was over.

36
After the News

Now that Japan had officially lost the war, the process by which we'd surrender ourselves had to be determined.

Our commander, Major Takazuka, called a meeting with the remaining officers to discuss the surrender arrangements. We all waited anxiously, fearing we'd be ordered to commit mass suicide rather than surrender to the enemy.

However, the decision was unexpected – we were to surrender to the Americans. The news filled me with mixed emotions.

We were told to head to the surrender location. We moved in small groups, barely able to walk. We had almost no food and no salt. Everyone was suffering and fighting off starvation.

One day, a high-ranking officer took food from a lower-ranking soldier.

"The war is over," I said. "We lost. Now all that matters is getting home to our families. We're all sick, but that soldier is worse off than you. Don't take his food. Go find your own like the rest of us. Rank doesn't matter anymore."

After a pause, he said, "You're still holding a grudge against me because of how I treated you during your training, aren't you?"

Back when I was a new recruit, he'd been in charge of training. He was strict and often picked on me more than the others. I'd always wondered if it was on purpose, maybe to test me. It became clear that he, too, had been aware of how he'd treated me. Seeing him now, in extreme deprivation, reminded me how war can bring out the true character of people.

Then he begged, "I can't find food on my own. Please help me."

"This isn't about the past," I answered. "I'll say what I need to say once we're both home. I'm not in perfect health either but I'm in better shape than you. I'll do my best to find food for myself. If I have any leftovers, I'll give them to you."

He nodded. "Okay, just let me eat something. Please," he begged again.

From then on, I worked even harder to gather food. If I had extra, I gave it to him.

One day, as we were passing through the mountains, we came across a small hut. Suddenly, I heard someone calling, "Riku-san! Riku-san!" This was a nickname navy soldiers used for army soldiers – it meant 'Mr Land'. I looked up and saw two navy officers coming out of the hut – men I'd worked with when I helped the navy construction team build anti-tank bombs months ago at the so-called 'Navy Hamlet' in Sarangani.

They said, "Mr. Kawabata, take some *shio* (salt) with you."

At first, I misunderstood them and said, "I already have *hi* (fire)." The two men were from the Kanto or Tohoku region, and I'd always struggled to distinguish their pronunciation of 'shi' and 'hi', hence my misunderstanding.

At that time, fire was just as precious as food. We had no matches, so we kept a corn cob ember burning, protecting it while walking, to start new fires with dry leaves. Sometimes we used a lens from broken binoculars to focus sunlight and light a fire – although this method rarely worked in the dark jungle.

"Shio! Shio!" they called again and gave me a bowl made from a coconut shell. It was filled with salt. Receiving such an unexpected and rare treasure moved me so much that tears streamed down my face. The gift of salt didn't just save my life – it saved the lives of everyone walking with me.

By then, none of us looked like real soldiers anymore. Some of us wore hats made from cloth scraps. Others had no hats at all. We had unshaven beards and our hair was thinning from malnourishment. In our mid-twenties, we looked nothing like the vigorous young men we were just a few years earlier.

Some of my close friends died around that time. Matsujiro Morita and Noboru Kagawa used up all their strength and passed away. Another, Shinichi Nishino, became too weak to walk and had to be carried on a wooden panel. One evening, we were camping in a raised-floor hut that belonged to a local villager. Too exhausted to lift Nishino up, we left him resting under the floor. When we checked on him at dawn, he'd passed away; his nose, ears and mouth already filled with ants.

Nishino had survived an earlier ordeal when our ship was bombed by American planes off the coast of Surigao. We'd rescued him and Kouichi Iwamoto after they'd swum ashore. Iwamoto died later in a field hospital. Nishino had stayed with us throughout the rest of the war, only to die just before we surrendered to the Americans.

I was heartbroken. I knew we were at war, but nothing prepared me for what I was seeing. A flood of emotions surged within me – sorrow, anger – and I had no means to express them. I think it was around the middle of September.

For five more days, we struggled down the mountains, fighting hunger, enduring the rain and suffering from malaria-induced fever.

At last, we arrived at the designated surrender point near the Klinan River crossing.

37

Surrender

Across the river, strong and healthy American soldiers with rosy cheeks were waiting next to trucks. They stood with their rifles in their muscular arms, which were thicker than our thighs. They looked well-fed and clean.

In contrast, we looked like skeletons wearing rags, with patchy hair and no shoes. We bore no resemblance to the young men who'd set off on this expedition just three or four years earlier, cheered on with shouts of encouragement, and full of spirit and vitality.

We crossed the shallow river and lined up. Our rifles, swords and grenades were, of course, confiscated and piled in one spot. After that, all personal clothing and belongings were thoroughly searched. Only items deemed non-threatening were returned. From me, they took a small pair of sewing scissors that had been a gift from my co-workers when I joined the army. The scissors had been incredibly useful, and I'd taken care not to lose them despite our countless relocations. In fact, they'd become like a good luck charm, so it was deeply disappointing to have them confiscated.

After the search had finished, we were packed tightly into the cargo beds of the trucks. We travelled over a vast grassy plain. It was rough and whenever the truck lurched forward all of us at the rear were thrown around. The American soldiers showed no concern, jeering at us as we fell, and the driver only sped up.

One soldier lit a cigarette, took a few puffs, then pretended to offer it to us. When people reached out, he smirked, threw the cigarette off the truck and burst into laughter. For the first time, I felt a deep sense of humiliation. He wore a gleaming gold wristwatch that was steadily ticking away. That watch seemed to represent everything America had that we didn't.

We reached a beach – probably Dadiangas on Sarangani Bay. This was where we had been stationed a few months earlier when we'd been forced to retreat under heavy American attack. We'd fought and lost many friends here. Now, under the tropical sun, the coastline looked peaceful. There was no sign of the fierce battles that had taken place, and gentle waves lapped the shore as if all the violence and death were from a distant past.

An American soldier shouted instructions in English but none of us understood. I listened carefully and gathered that he was explaining how to set up the tents, where to cook and how food would be supplied. I explained to the others. We received our first rations from the Americans and made a simple meal.

That night, we set up our tents on the soft beach sand. I stretched out my legs and lay down. My mind was full of the faces of the friends we had lost – ghostly, emaciated and hollow-eyed as they used the last of their strength to descend the mountains. I couldn't sleep.

Eventually, I started to doze off but was jolted awake by three American soldiers. They searched through my few remaining possessions, then pointed a gun at me and pulled the trigger. It wasn't loaded. It was just to scare me. They made me take off my clothes, thinking I was hiding something valuable. Even though they came from a rich country, these soldiers still acted like bullies when placed in the lawless environment.

The next morning, several small Landing Ship Tanks (LSTs) arrived on the beach to pick us up. A crowd of local people had already gathered. They were angry – shouting at us and throwing things. Some pointed at individuals, accusing them of specific wrongdoings. At that moment, anyone could be seen as the enemy. We tried not to stand out. Some of us hid behind others, covered our faces with bags or rubbed dirt on our faces so no-one would recognise us as we walked quickly to the ships.

Just before I boarded, an American soldier grabbed my arm and said, "Officer." I quickly answered, "No! I am a soldier." He let go and I was allowed to board the ship. He must have assumed I was an officer because I'd explained the tent setup and food distribution to my comrades, giving directions the previous day on the beach.

Later, some of my friends asked, "What did he say to you?" I told them and they looked surprised. "Why didn't you say yes? Officers get better treatment – maybe better food!"

Later, however, we found out the officers were taken somewhere else for strict interrogation. They didn't get to go home until much later than we soldiers did. I was glad I'd told the truth.

Our ship headed south across the bright blue water of Sarangani Bay. As the shoreline faded into the distance, the mountains and jungles where we'd endured countless days of danger, hardship and suffering began to look strangely nostalgic. I felt a quiet sorrow, knowing I would never return to that place. Tears welled up as I thought of the many friends buried there. Two massive dead trees, which had always marked our way back to camp no matter where we went, now stood gleaming under the tropical sun, as if silently seeing us off.

38
Prisoner-of-War Camp

While I was lost in my memories of Sarangani, we arrived at a coastline far from Davao. There, we were immediately transferred to amphibious vehicles. They took us to a prisoner-of-war camp set up at the base of a low mountain, away from the shore.

The camp had five fenced-in areas. Each one had about fifty tents and was surrounded by barbed wire with American guards stationed at the corners. Officers and higher ranks were kept in a different area. The rest of us – soldiers from both the army and navy – were put together. There were eight of us in a tent meant for two American soldiers with beds. We slept on the ground so it wasn't too crowded.

None of the provisions – clothing, food or shelter – were enough, but what troubled us most were shoes. Most of us were barefoot or wore barely-there handmade sandals. The American forces gave us used military shoes, for which I was especially grateful as I needed a large size.

By chance, one of my tentmates was Master Sergeant Seiichi Fujisaki, who I'd known at headquarters. There were also two men from Korea and four younger soldiers. Later, the Korean men were taken away – I don't know where they went. After that, the room became more spacious, shared among just six of us.

Coincidentally, across from our tent were eight navy soldiers. Two of them were the ones who had given me the precious salt during our surrender march through the jungle. Overjoyed to reunite, we celebrated each other's survival and maintained our friendship throughout our time in the camp.

That same day, we were each taken into a tent for questioning. A Japanese-American soldier asked us questions and wrote our names on prisoner cards.

Next to our camp was another group of prisoners who'd been captured earlier. They wore American clothes marked with big letters: 'P • W' (Prisoner-of-War). We heard they were treated well as heroes who'd contributed to peace by giving up early.

In our camp, we received two meals a day – American military rations – and sometimes even a cup of milk. Almost every day, one person from each tent would go with an American soldier to pick fruit, like pomelos, to add to our meals. Two or three people from each tent were also sent out each day for random tasks. Some of the tasks were okay, but others were very hard or unpleasant.

Every day at a set time, we gathered near the guard post, got into trucks or amphibious vehicles, and were taken to different places for work. If we were taken into the mountains, we knew we'd have to cut down trees – a job we all disliked because it was physically exhausting. If we went along flat roads towards an American base, the jobs were lighter, like cleaning kitchens or scrubbing equipment. But even those weren't pleasant. While we worked and sweated, American soldiers nearby would play cards and drink whiskey.

One day, I was told to clean a bread oven. It was covered in grease and soot. An American soldier threw me his clean uniform to use as a cleaning rag. It was nicer than the clothes I had on! When I started to change into it, a big man nearby turned red and yelled, "*Kitanai*!" (dirty). He was very upset and insisted I had to use the clean uniform to do the dirty work instead.

Sometimes we were sent to the beach. If we were lucky, we got to work in the food warehouse. It was huge and was filled with all sorts of supplies. From the front, everything looked neat and tidy, but in the back many boxes had already been opened, with much of their contents stolen or missing.

High-demand, easy-to-carry items, like sultanas, were a prized find. We'd hide them in our boots and bring them back to camp to share. If the guards caught us taking food, the black American guards were usually more forgiving than the white ones. They would just tell us to stop and send us to another job.

Occasionally, funny things happened, such as the time one of the prisoners was caught red-handed, with sultanas in his mouth. A black American guard shouted, "Come on!" to warn him. However, the prisoner thought he said *kamawan* (which means 'it's okay' in Japanese) and kept eating until he got caught by another patrol and scolded severely.

As the days went by, we began to wonder how long we'd be stuck there. Speculation ran wild. Some said, "We'll be sent home before New Year's." Others said, "Don't be so optimistic. We surrendered. They'll send us to Alaska to work and then be secretly killed." Some said we'd be taken to Okinawa to help rebuild and then be set free.

At the beginning of November, a jeep with three or four American soldiers came to the guard post. One was a Japanese-American. They had lists of names. They called out names and told those people to pack their belongings and get ready to leave the next morning.

The people whose names were called left with mixed feelings – nervous but also hopeful. A few days later, more names were called. Some of the people from my tent left too.

Eventually, everyone in my tent had gone and the nearby empty tents were dismantled.

Luckily, the navy men in the tent across from mine were still there. They were kind to me and kept me company.

At night, lying alone in the now spacious tent, I couldn't help but wonder why I was being left behind. I stared at the moon in the clear night sky through the tent's entrance, its beauty only deepening my sadness. Tears flowed silently as I lay awake.

A few days later, the jeep came again. As usual, they read names. This time, it seemed they were only calling navy men, so I went back to my tent and tried to nap.

Suddenly, one of the navy officers burst in and said, "Mr Kawabata! Hurry! They just called your name!" I jumped up and ran to the guard post.

The Japanese-American soldier lightly slapped me and scolded, "Where have you been? Don't you want to go back to Japan?" He told me to get ready to leave the next morning.

I clearly heard the words 'go back to Japan'. Overjoyed, I returned to the tent and began packing my few belongings. I was too excited to sleep that night.

The navy soldiers from the tent in front of mine also received their orders that morning.

39

Coming Home

The next morning, we gathered in front of the camp as instructed. After roll call, we got into trucks and were taken to the beach. When we arrived, we put on a life jacket and got into amphibious vehicles, with the guards making sure the seating limit was adhered to. The vehicle sped across the beach, entered the sea and headed towards a ship anchored offshore.

These vehicles had been used before to transport us for work assignments. Back then, they packed us in tightly with no regard for safety. Yet here, despite still being prisoners-of-war, they gave us life jackets and made sure we weren't overcrowded. It was a small act, but I felt it showed a measure of respect and decency on America's part.

Before long, we arrived at the mothership – an approximately 10,000-tonne cargo ship – and were split into groups. Some stayed in the front hold and some in the back. We weren't allowed to move between the two. In the middle of the ship were the American soldiers and crew. They had guards watching us all the time.

Most of the prisoners on board were navy men. There weren't many army soldiers like me. Ship duties, like cleaning, were led by navy officers and carried out efficiently. They joked with me, saying, "Riku-san, you're just getting in the way!" and allowed me to pass the voyage with relatively little to do.

We still received two meals a day, just like in the camp. I wasn't hungry, though. The lack of physical exercise and the relaxed atmosphere on the ship dulled my appetite. I was also seasick throughout the journey. Even two meals a day felt like too much.

When we'd been making our way to the Philippines, I hadn't had time for seasickness. Back then, we'd lived in the ship's hold alongside horses, and had constantly been under threat from enemy attacks and pushing through gruelling tasks.

But now, on the peaceful voyage home and with the war over, I was not only physically weaker but also in a relaxed mind state – both enough to contribute to feeling seasick.

To stay healthy, we were allowed to go up on the deck for a little while each morning and evening. In the morning, we washed our faces. In the evening, during the brief twilight, we used open-air toilets – makeshift wooden boxes that were shaped like a 'U' and had seawater constantly flowing through them. There we'd sit, lined up like sparrows on a telephone wire, relieving ourselves in the gusty sea wind.

After several uneventful days at sea, I felt the wind change. One morning, looking out across the ocean, I glimpsed land in the distance. It was Taiwan. The sight assured me that I was nearing home.

A few days later, early in the morning, we stepped out onto the deck to an overcast sky and a misty horizon. And there, like a pencil line drawn across the grey canvas, stood the unmistakable silhouette of Mount Fuji.

It was Japan.

All of us gathered quietly on the deck, clenching our jaws, tears brimming, until finally, our silent crying turned into audible sobs.

As the day brightened under the crisp autumn sky, the ship drew closer to land and dropped anchor. The distant mountains bathed in blazing crimson autumn foliage were striking beyond words. Still unaware of the devastation awaiting us on shore, I recalled the line from an old Chinese poem: *The country is broken, yet mountains and rivers remain.*

The ship anchored just off the Port of Uraga on the Miura Peninsula and we stayed onboard for another night. The next morning, we were transferred to a small wooden barge and finally set foot on Japanese soil.

The ruined state of our country that greeted us far exceeded anything we'd imagined. It was the raw reality of a lost war. As we walked through the charred remains of Uraga, we felt the cold stares from passersby. We were guided to the barracks of the former Army Transport Academy, where we stayed for about five days to finish paperwork and, then, return to civilian life.

On the 25th of November 1945, I arrived at the fire-ravaged Osaka Station around noon, after an overnight journey on a slow local train.

I'd finally returned home.

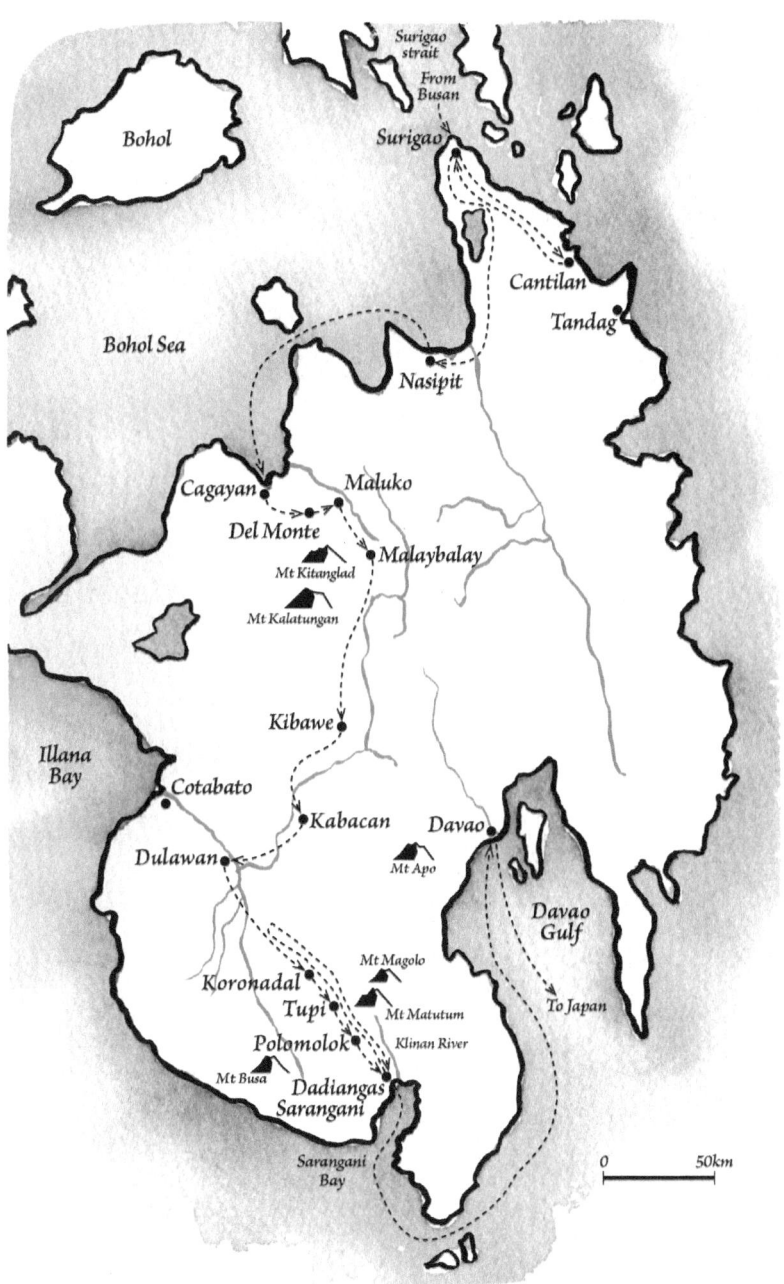

Our movements on Mindanao Island

40

Afterword

I first started writing this memoir on a whim. I just picked up a pen and began.

However, over half a century had passed and in many places my memories had grown faint. I was especially unsure of dates and locations and, more than once, I considered giving up the project altogether.

Each time, however, I reminded myself why I'd started. I pushed through, relying on my best judgement, and gradually put together my experience – from the day I was drafted on the 1st of February 1942 to the day I returned home on the 25th of November 1945.

To fill in the gaps in my memories, particularly regarding dates and places, I referred to the anthology

Minpyō (Sleeping Leopard), published for the 17th Memorial of the Leopard Unit on the 27th of August 1961, as well as *Memories of the 30th Division (Leopard Army Corps)*, published on the 6th of September 1981.

Even after finishing, I kept remembering more. Maybe someday, I'll write another book with those missing parts – maybe I'll call it *Sketches from the Battlefield*.

Our precious youth was taken from us. We were thrown into a war that never should have happened. We fought against our enemies, and against hunger and disease. Ultimately, we fought against ourselves – in hardship and in desperate struggle. By what can only be described as one miracle after another, I was fortunate enough to return home alive. For us, it was a horrible war, yet what we went through left a deep mark on who we became.

What's really disappointing is that none of our leaders left behind any written records of this 'precious war history'. When my memory was unclear, I had to rely on documents written by those outside the unit to verify basic facts, such as dates and locations.

Back then, our Prime Minister, General Hideki Tōjō, made all soldiers memorise a harsh set of rules.

One said: *A soldier must never suffer the shame of being captured. Die rather than be taken alive.*

Yet when the war ended, he himself hesitated to take his own life; instead, he was captured by the Americans and subsequently executed.

There is no uglier vanity than that of a leader who, while advocating suicide to avoid the shame of capture, could not carry it out himself when the time came.

More than half a century has passed. Japan has achieved remarkable economic development and, today, its people live well-fed, well-dressed and in peace. But I wonder: can we, the generation who experienced the war, say that we are truly content?

It feels as though we now live in an era rich in material goods but poor in spirit. For those of us who sacrificed our youth, endured unbearable hardship and were lucky enough to return home alive, what has been the reward?

The spotlight now shines on the frivolous parts of society.

Most of all, I feel deep sorrow for the many comrades who endured starvation, suffered from disease, spent the last of their strength and perished in the jungles of Mindanao in the Philippines.

20th of August 1996

My sister (left), my grandfather, and I (right)

Acknowledgements

I want to thank my husband, Cem Ozturk, for his endless support, for helping with the first edit of my rough translation, and for guiding me with English nuances along the way.

I am also grateful to my parents for digging into old documents to help clarify our family history for this book.

Finally, I'm thankful to Kellie Nissen for her thoughtful edits and kind guidance through this process.

This book would not have been possible without you. Thank you for helping me carry my grandfather's stories into the future.

www.ingramcontent.com/pod-product-compliance
Lightning Source LLC
Chambersburg PA
CBHW020529080526
44583CB00013B/798